Single 101

101 Reasons To
Celebrate Being Single

Designed by Celeste Friedman.
Library of Congress Cataloging- in- Publication data is available upon request.

ISBN-10:1451510519
EAN-13: 9781451510515

www.Single-101.blogspot.com

Single 101

101 Reasons To
Celebrate Being Single

CELESTE FRIEDMAN

Dedicated to hearts content with living outside of the mainstream, who discover more about themselves than they wouldn't have otherwise.

CONTENTS

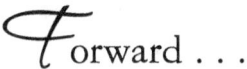orward . . .

After two marriages and a few live-in boyfriends, I developed a love-hate relationship with being single. I have passed on several career opportunities, been forced to sell my dream home that I built with my late father and given up much of what I've wished for, all due to my loyalty toward a spouse or lover.

I was a typical girl who dreamed of true love, my wedding day and a happy family. My first marriage evolved into a partnership which sadly grew apart due to opposing career goals. Religious differences and financial status tore my second marriage to shreds, as I was from a lower-class factory town with Gentile blood flowing in my veins.

By trade, I'm a singer-songwriter and composer. Realizing that I was sacrificing my career and catering exclusively to the demands of the men in my life, I had no choice but to throw in the towel. I walked away every time, starting all over again and again.

Once I gave myself the chance to focus on my own needs and my career, I became far more successful living alone. While staying single, I have been nominated for a Grammy Award; scored for a Pulitzer Prize-nominated play; won several awards in music and education; received award nominations for contributions in television; and given wonderful opportunities to write and perform for children.

I'll be the first to admit that it's complicated to live with me. My passion for writing and composing consumes my days, nights or both. I don't function well in a messy environment and prefer to have the bed all to myself.

Through the years I have been dealt a few bad cards, from three miscarriages to being struck with rheumatoid arthritis in the prime of my life, to site just two examples. There are times when I regret not being able to have children and wonder what life would be like now if I had a family.

Today, more men and women are planning and developing a career ahead of marriage. The general consensus for men seems to be the desire to build wealth and status first, where women want the freedom to establish themselves as individuals, gaining self respect and self worth. Statistics show that more people are choosing the single life after divorce or failed relationships.

In Single 101: 101 Reasons to Celebrate Being Single, my mission is to entertain, inspire and support both men and women who relish their independence. Single 101 upholds an individual's dignity; gives allegiance to those who choose to live single and encouragement to others considering the possibilities; and opens our eyes to the truth that not all people who are single have been abandoned, are lonely or desperate.

Single 101: 101 Reasons to Celebrate Being Single is a countdown to Number One. Living alone doesn't have to be a permanent situation. Many find it invaluable to experience total freedom for as long as they like. Remember Reason #30- You Rule!

Eventually, I gave in to the theory that it is far better to be alone than to wish you were. In my pursuit of happiness, I am content flying solo. My story is reflected in Reason Number One.

One final note:

Some people may pop open the champagne and literally celebrate, while others may find that the path they have paved for themselves as a single person is not what they had imagined.

If you are completely alone in life, aging with no children or family close by, I pray that you have dear friends and compassionate neighbors. It is possible to reach a point where living all alone forces you to find a new living arrangement, should you lack the resources to survive or have a threatening health issue. Freedom is not free.

Hopefully you are blessed with independence and peace for a long, long time.

Best wishes,

$\mathcal{C}$eleste

Spontaneity

The choice to fly solo can even be a spontaneous intention and one that you may never regret. Even if you find that the single life is not for you, the opportunity that you give yourself to explore the possibilities is a worthy journey.

Each day begins with decisions that you make on your own. Whether it's household chores or ways to pass the time, there is no reason to need permission for anything. You come and go as you please, day or night.

In today's world of juggling work and leisure, spontaneity has fallen low on the list of simple pleasures, but single living affords more chances to do whatever you'd like at the spur of the moment.

If you could do something spontaneous right now, what would it be? How many times have you claimed to have almost done something spontaneous? Wouldn't it be wild to jump out of your car on Highway 405 in Los Angeles, lock the door and start walking around, saying hello to everyone else who's stuck in traffic with you? Who knows who you would meet?

Singer-songwriter Paul Simon once wrote:
> *"Improvisation is too good to leave to chance."*

*Y*ou Can Live Anywhere You Like

Reason #100

Have you ever wished that you lived in an exotic place or simply just somewhere else? If given the opportunity and depending upon your responsibilities, a single person can pack up and move across town or over the ocean at the drop of a hat, without the complexities of a spouse's career needs or family ties.

Money Magazine released a list of the best smallest cities in America in 2007. According to their research, Ohio is the best in the Midwest for small communities with populations between 7,500 and 50,000 with the lowest crime rate and home affordability, in addition to high rankings in racial diversity, health care access, arts and leisure.

In 1989, Seattle was voted as the Number One best city to live in America, where Puget Sound, Mount Rainier and the Cascade Mountains make you forget about how much it rains there.

State College, Pennsylvania and Durham, New Hampshire are college towns where 75% of the population is single. Steeped in history, architecture and romantic landscapes, these serene, cozy communities thrive with plenty of entertainment and nightlife.

The Number One city in the world to live in, according to Traveler's Digest, is Montreal, Canada. It's one of the most diverse cultural cities with a growing economy. Just plan on gearing up with plenty of fleece, corduroys and mittens and learn to speak Francais!

Now, close your eyes and point your finger to somewhere on the map. Then, open your eyes and discover your future destination.

*M*ore Job Opportunities

You can take any job offer without having to worry about how your career needs will affect someone else.

Since Evan was 25, he has been determined to remain open to all possibilities. You never know what offer is going to come your way and when it does, you have to be ready for it. He knows that if he had a wife and children right now, it would be very complicated to accept a good offer, especially when striving to climb up the corporate ladder. Not every family can just pack up and go, making sacrifices for the sake of one's new job. When Evan thinks of the house hunting, searching for the right school, a safe neighborhood, a spouse's career, it's too much to handle all at once.

Evan's girlfriend moved in with him a year ago. They were doing okay and pretty happy living a great life in Chicago. Two months later, he received an offer to relocate to Atlanta. His girlfriend was unable to find a comparable job there and they agreed to split up. She's still in Chicago doing well and he's in San Francisco now. Atlanta was only a stepping stone, but a necessary move for his career.

So, they both survived, but lived through a long, heartbreaking period of time that neither ever wish to repeat.

You Don't Have to Worry if He Will or Won't Call

Reason #98

We've all been there, wondering if he's going to call and when. Most of us would love to have a 'Get Out of Limbo' ticket. *"Where can I get one?"* you might ask.

It was a gloomy, rainy day, of course. Michaela had just interviewed for a great job with a fashion manufacturer, who said they would contact her by the end of the week. She desperately wanted this job, needed more money and the wardrobe comps were exceptionally generous. The interview was on a Tuesday. But let's move on to Wednesday.

Michaela had been dating Tim for almost a year. He was notorious for never calling, so she always found herself being the more assertive partner in the relationship. Tim seemed happy for her that she'd finally landed the interview and she moped around her apartment all of Wednesday, wishing that he'd at least call and ask how it went.

"What does he do all the time?" she thought. *"Is he sitting around hoping I'll call or maybe just thinking that I'll call eventually, so he won't worry about it?"* Watching out the window at the pouring rain, she made a promise to herself that she would not call him. She wanted to see if he really cared about her.

After finishing off half a bag of potato chips, she stopped in front of the refrigerator. Staring at the freezer door, she came close to having a feast with what was left of the chocolate chip ice cream. Instead, she broke the promise she had made to herself and grabbed the phone. She called Tim and got his voicemail, but didn't leave a message. An hour later, she tried his cell phone and left a short message, just saying that it was her calling. Shoveling the ice cream into her mouth, she began to get angry that Tim never offered her emotional support and decided not to dare call him again or answer the phone if it rang.

Around 3:30, Wednesday afternoon, the phone rang a couple of times, but she let the voicemail capture the calls. So furious with not only Tim, but herself for being so weak, she decided not to check the messages. Assuming that she wouldn't hear from the employer until Friday, she was certain that if the phone actually rang, it would either be Tim or her mother.

Michaela finally checked the messages later on Thursday to learn that she'd missed her opportunity for the new position. It was the employer who had called twice. Their messages stated that they had experienced such an unbelievable response to the job opening, they would need to hear back from her by 5:00pm that day, otherwise the position would go to the second most valuable candidate.

Her obsession over Tim cost her the new job. That was Thursday and by Friday, Tim had still never called.

The Crossword Puzzle Is All Yours!

I suppose you can blame it all on Joseph Pulitzer, who published the very first crossword puzzle in his publication, The New York World, on December 21, 1913. Arthur Wynne, who created the puzzle in the shape of a diamond with just a few clues, started a phenomenon that many newspaper subscribers cannot live without to this day. Many newspaper publishers will tell you that you can forget to post an important news item with no reaction, but if you fail to publish the daily crossword puzzle, readers will have a snit.

According to Will Shortz, editor of the New York Times crossword puzzle, as many as 50 million people do crossword puzzles just in the United States alone. One reader claims that he never gets bored as long as he has his daily puzzle, where another woman says that it keeps her mind sharp, improving her vocabulary.

A homemaker in Virginia states that she cringed when her husband bought her a crossword puzzle dictionary for Christmas, thinking it would help her. *"That would be cheating,"* she said. But hold everything! If you're having trouble getting that last word, you can actually have your clues analyzed at www.OneAcross.com. In the event that you get stuck, OneAcross.com will help you out and no one is the wiser.

Rumors and tales have spread throughout the last century that some marriages have become stronger and some have failed because of the addiction to crossword puzzles. Have a score to settle or a little vendetta? Just hide the enemy's crossword puzzle!

Hazel Warren of London, England claims that she actually forgot to prepare dinner for her family one night. Others like Hazel say they've been late picking up the kids from school or late for work, all because of the rage over 'Sudoku'. Sudoku, which means 'single number' in Japanese, is essentially a simple logic problem with layers of hidden complexity that can draw the solver in to the point of obsession. They claim it's all the rage in the UK.

Isn't it lovely to be single? You have the freedom to sort out the logical assumptions on your own, celebrate your prowess of completing the puzzle yourself and you never have to argue or debate over your choices. If you can't take the puzzle with you, it will still be there in the safe place where you left it when you return home.

$\mathcal{Y}$ou Can Eat Garlic and Onions with No Need for Breath Mints

Here's a great recipe for fun and good health:

White Rice with Garlic, Onions & Vegetables

Ingredients
>   11 tablespoons of olive oil
>   1/2 medium onion, chopped
>   2 cloves minced garlic
>   2 cups of long grain rice
>   4 cups of hot water
>   1/2 teaspoon salt
>   1/2 cup of peas, carrots or peppers

Preparation
In a medium pan, sauté onion, garlic, and rice in olive oil.
Add hot water and salt.

Bring to a full boil. Cover and simmer for 15 minutes
without stirring. If desired, add vegetables, cover, and cook
for an additional five minutes.

Uncover, give rice a full turn, and cover again. Turn heat off.
Let stand 15 minutes before serving.

*Y*ou Can Be Happy with Who You Are and Not Who He Wants You to Be

Reason #95

When you lay your head on your pillow tonight, will you be happy with who you are? As you reflect on the day, are you pleased with your life and how you live it?

Maria and her husband were married for seven years. In the beginning, it seemed as though he loved everything about her, but after a year, things began to change. *"Maybe I took it for granted at first that he was happy with me, since he always appeared to be,"* she thought.

During the pregnancy of their first child, he began to criticize Maria's appearance. No matter how she dressed or wore her hair, he wasn't satisfied. She knew that he was actually embarrassed to be seen in public with her, as the size of her tummy increased more and more. After their daughter was born, she joined an aerobics class, watched her diet and returned to the former weight that she'd maintained before they were married. However, he continued to be critical of her appearance.

He was discontent with the clothes she bought for their little girl and demanded she return them to the store. One evening, he complained about her cooking, saying that he'd just put up with it over the years and finally had to say something. After their second child was born, Maria did her best to keep the toys and play areas organized, but for her husband, their house was never tidy enough.

After five years with this man, Maria fell out of love with him. She began to hate herself and accepted the blame for everything. One morning after taking her daughter to school, she packed up the baby and went to the library. She found a huge section of self-help books and started to research what was wrong with her. The library became an obsession, as she couldn't get enough information. Maria rapidly learned that the problem wasn't her after all.

Each day she felt stronger and more confident to face her husband when he would badger and ridicule. She finally mustered up the courage to leave him, found legal counsel, filed for divorce and got custody of her children.

Maria would like to re-marry someday, but she's enjoying her freedom too much. There's actually more time that she can devote to her children and so much more time for herself. She loves and respects who she sees in the mirror!

You Can Have Sexual Gratification Anytime You Desire

Jordan is a nurse, working in the ER of a busy hospital. After graduation, she met Nathan, an intern who worked on the same night shift. They began to date and moved in with each other one year later.

Jordan and Nathan had a very healthy and passionate sexual relationship in the beginning. Since they were on the same schedule, they were able to have a lot of fun together off the clock. About two months after they moved into their apartment, Nathan's schedule was changed and he began to go on duty as Jordan was going off at 7:30 in the morning. From time to time, they would rendezvous in the nurses' supply closet or he would take a lunch break and come home when she was trying to sleep, which became difficult for her.

Eventually, they hardly ever saw each other and grew apart. One day Nathan told her that he was disenchanted with their sexual relationship and that he was having more fun in the shower alone with his right hand than with her. She was shocked to hear him make such a condescending remark and it was his schedule that had changed their routine to begin with. Their relationship evolved into how important it was to please Nathan, regardless of how Jordan felt or what she needed.

Jordan kept it to herself that she had also struggled with feeling sexually satisfied with Nathan. When he moved out, she finally realized that whether you're in a relationship or not, you don't have to abstain from satisfying your own desires.

You Can Have Male Friends without Defending Yourself

Reason #93

Are you free to make friends with whomever you want, especially the opposite sex? Here are two stories from women who struggled with this issue . . .

Cherie lives on the Atlantic coast of Florida, where the beach is only two blocks from her condo. She frequents the beach to walk along the shoreline, feed the gulls and listen to the ocean. One afternoon, her boyfriend Chad confronted her about how late she was getting home. She told him that she ran into a friend and didn't mean to be late.

Chad became suspicious and allowed his imagination to run wild. Late one afternoon, he stopped by the beach and saw Cherie sitting on a bench having a conversation with a man he didn't recognize. Chad approached them and asked Cherie if she was ready to go home. She paused to introduce Chad to the man on the bench, when Chad interrupted and insisted they leave immediately.

"What is your problem, Chad?" she asked, as they walked toward the car. *"So, is this where you go to meet men?"* he yelled back. Cherie's jaw dropped. She reminded Chad that she had female and male friends and if he had a problem with that, he'd better think twice about living with her.

Alena works at a health club, where both co-workers and members are male. There was a time when she was struggling with not only a jealous husband, but a co-worker who had been flirting with her. As she found herself constantly re-assuring her husband that she wasn't interested in anyone at work, she was also being confronted by her jealous boss, every time he thought she was being too flirtatious with male members of the club.

"It was a nightmare," said Alena, "a very difficult time in my life. I love my husband, but he has never accepted how I have to dress at the club and who our employees interact with there".

$\mathcal{F}$ree Drinks in Pubs and Clubs

Being unattached when you're partying in pubs and nightclubs can make it easier if you're trolling for a free daiquiri or beer. Whether it's Happy Hour, Ladies Night or a free drink for singing karaoke, there are more places you can imagine where the booze is flowing freely.

It's also amazing to learn how many women have this thing down to a science. Even if they don't admit to mooching off of friends and their favorite bartender, they're very organized right down to the hors-d'oeuvres at wine tastings. Just how easy is it?

A few of my girlfriends have a weekly calendar, called their 'party-time schedule'. Monday nights are specifically for ridding their woes of the typical manic Monday at the office. Jordan's Harbour Pub gets the evening started with free goodies on the buffet and a complimentary flute of wine. For just the girls, it has to be pink on Mondays, so the Zinfandel is perfect.

Skipping to Wednesdays, the hot karaoke spot is Mandy's, where the free cocktails keep flowing for the one who is the most popular singer. If the audience keeps voting for that singer, one can have all the imported beer or wine of their choice!

Every other Thursday night they head out to Moe's Sports Bar, where it's Ladies Night. Ladies get in free and the first drink is on the house. Everyone is always checking out ring fingers, even though that doesn't seem to matter anymore. They offer free salsa lessons, where the main room cuts loose and gets wild.

Fridays are a must at Club 21. They have a great deejay and the ladies get two free drinks before 10:00pm, plus no cover charge. If they're partying into the weekend, Shenanigans' downtown offers a Girl's Classic Card, where ladies can drink free Long Island Ice Teas from 9:30pm on into the night on Saturday nights.

There are some who contest the whole principle behind Ladies Night. If women can receive a free drink, many men believe they should have the same benefit. One man actually filed a lawsuit against several night spots promoting Ladies Night. His attorney in Manhattan stated, *"An establishment that offers Ladies Night enticements, violates the 14th Amendment's guarantee of equal protection under the law"*.

The class action suit accuses several New York City clubs of 'invidious discrimination' against men in their policies for admitting patrons. This is one man's fight over clubs who, in his words, *"discriminate against men"*.

*Y*ou Can Flirt As Much As You Want

Some agree that coquetry is truly an art form. Here are a few tips from today's dating experts:

Give Clear Signals
Since your intensions can be easily misconstrued, make sure that you are sincere and clear with who you choose to flirt with and be cautious of how far you intend to go.

Go It Alone
If you're out with a group of friends, separate yourself from them if you want to be more approachable. No one is going to flirt with someone who is protected by their posse.

Be In Good Voice
If you laugh like a hyena or speak so softly where no one can barely hear a word you're saying, your flirting techniques won't have a chance. Speak clearly with a pleasant voice and don't waste your time yelling in someone's ear if the music is too loud.

Use Proper Rejection Etiquette
If approached by someone who grosses you out, be polite and move on. Unless they relentlessly hover and won't leave you alone, you can still find stronger ways of getting your point across, rather than saying, *"Get lost loser!"*

Leave Your Ego at the Door
Hold the chatter about yourself and ask him or her about them. Flattery just may get you somewhere.

Can I Have Your Number?
If you carry a personal or business card, this is best. Don't waste someone's time with a fake number. Be genuine if you're seriously interested.

It's How You Play the Game
Many men will admit that they'd enjoy being approached by a woman. Give it a try and watch what happens.

Be Yourself
Life is too short to lie or make up stories about your life or career. Keep it simple and be proud of who you are. If you feel you need to be protective at first, you can talk about what you do without divulging the name of the company you own or work for.

Dress for Success
Your appearance will be the key to how successful your flirting attempts will be, whether it's your hair, what you're wearing or even your accessories. Some women say they carry something just to get noticed. Is that how the miniature dog thing got started with Paris Hilton?

You Are at the Controls

When birth control pills first arrived on the scene, there was one brand. Now it's no different than buying cereal. Some people only need to prevent pregnancy, where others want to protect themselves or their partners from sexually transmitted diseases.

Your choice of birth control should depend on several factors. These include your health, frequency of sexual activity, number of sexual partners and the desire to have children. Your health care provider can help you select the best form of birth control for you, but it all comes down to you to ensure your own sexual well being.

In today's world, thank goodness for the Internet. Check out BirthControl.com. We've come a long, long way in just the past twenty years. With a variety of oral contraceptives, condoms, IUD's, spermicides, implants, patches, rings, caps, diaphragms, douches, vasectomy procedures, even the rhythm method, it can make you dizzy just thinking about it.

Your family doctor can inform you about the pros and cons of each birth control option, but he or she doesn't have the time to consult you on those specifics. It's your responsibility to do the research. Few doctors will take the time to provide printed materials on in-depth research and potential side effects. You must ask them if they provide literature.

There are many serious factors to consider: your heart, decrease in bone density, nausea, depression, weight gain and the list goes on. In totality, it is your body and you have the wheel.

"I celebrate myself and sing myself."
... Walt Whitman

You Can Hang Your Unmentionables Wherever You Choose

Reason #89

The stockings may hang by the chimney with care at Christmastime, but on a daily basis, your unmentionables may be unwanted articles hanging to dry in the bathroom.

In many a quaint village in Europe, where one tenant building stands inches from the next, you can still find laundry, including the lingerie hanging out to dry on the clotheslines, tied between the downspouts. It's funny to see, but I hope they never change!

Men foam at the mouth when they see us wearing push up bras, thongs, garter belts and seamed stockings, but dislike where we choose to hang them up to dry. If you're single and living alone, your delicates can dry on the back of the kitchen chair or tossed over the shower curtain without a care.

A friend of mine always keeps her racing bike inside her apartment, parked near a heating vent. It isn't unusual to see her bras or stockings hanging from the handle bars.

So, what's that tucked inside your little pink striped bag? I'll never tell.

$\mathcal{M}$ore Opportunities to Meet New People

Ladies, I hear you loud and clear- you don't pick up men in bars and clubs. C'mon, think outside of the box and seek out new venues.

Here are one dozen great places to meet new friends:
1. Health Clubs
2. Museums
3. Single's Groups
4. Events: Sporting, Wine Tasting or Meetups
5. Networking Groups
6. Book Clubs
7. Civic Organizations
8. Neighborhood Watch Programs
9. Volunteer Organizations and Churches
10. Workshops and Seminars
11. Parties
12. Resorts and Spas

It's amazing how many wonderful people you meet traveling, even if it's a few miles from your own front door. If you travel to a new country, you can also learn about a different culture or how to speak a new language. I'll guarantee that you'll come home with names and addresses of new pen pals.

How would you like to find new friends who are into enlightenment and spiritual well being? Step into the light and sign up for a yoga or tai chi class. Aaah! Just the sound of the word, 'yoga' is relaxing.

Go shopping, even if you have no money, browse and window shop. You may find a new friend in a pet store or the local humane society. Which reminds me . . . lots of dog lovers will tell you to just get a dog, go to the park or the beach and watch what happens! (Instant friends and so much fun!) Besides, your cat wouldn't be very happy at the beach anyway.

Assert yourself. It's easier than you think to bag that shy side of your personality and start opening up to new people. Talk to strangers who are friendly in appearance. It makes waiting in line at the market go so much faster.

Last but not least, smile at someone when you pass them on the street and by all means, smile back at someone who has smiled at you. What a gift!

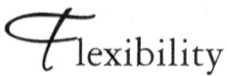

Flexibility

Living single allows you countless perks that you wouldn't have if you were married or in a relationship. If someone calls out of the blue and wants to meet for coffee, you can drop what you're doing and go. If your golfing buddy calls and says he just booked a tee time and it has your name on it, you can grab your clubs without having to make sure if it's okay with someone else.

You can say, *"yes"* so much more, instead of those tired old answers like, *"I don't know"*, *"I'll have to check with so and so"*, *"It's just not a good idea right now"* or *"I have to wait until my husband gets home to watch the kids"*.

There are probably millions of people who will claim that their lives are not that rigid, but if you knew the real truth, the only time they really feel flexible is in their yoga class. Consider the benefits if everyone could have more flexibility.

Think about it from an anatomical standpoint, where more range of motion and better circulation is rewarded from stretching and exercise. Imagine the benefits for our spirit and general well being!

*Y*ou Don't Have to Compromise

During the holidays, some of us enjoy a lovely, festive meal with dear ones and others are wishing they had figured out an excuse to get out of going in the first place.

Maggie was born and raised in the Midwestern United States, where it was tradition to stuff and roast a turkey. They had all the trimmings with potatoes, gravy, an assortment of cooked vegetables, cranberry relish, corn bread and pumpkin pie. She and her husband had been married for eighteen years, but he was never satisfied with Thanksgiving served at their house, where Maggie did all the cooking. He grew up in Maine, where the holidays were centered on his family's seafood business. Thanksgiving and Christmas to his family meant clam chowder or lobster bisque, fresh scallops, shrimp and anything seafood. Potatoes were acceptable, but cranberry relish came out of the can.

Not a seafood lover herself, she dreaded those long trips to the east coast every other year. Trying to be polite, Maggie would sip her chowder and get full on mashed potatoes. What she was most thankful for on those Thanksgiving excursions was simply the pumpkin pie!

Maggie isn't alone. Many of us can clash when it comes to taste, especially on such a day of feasting. The total win-win if you're single is that you can travel anywhere you want for the holidays, eat what you want, select what you want at the market or simply stay home and curl up with a great book.

Do you say, *"to-mah-to"* or *"to-may-to"?*

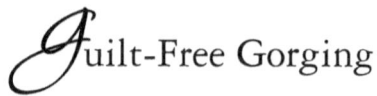uilt-Free Gorging

Reason # 85

As I write, the snow is continuing to fall on top of the three feet already on the ground. The local meteorologists have already named this the blizzard of the year and winter isn't finished with us yet.

Our local post office has made the decision to break their *'Whether rain, snow, sleet or hail, the mail will get through'* promise and postpone mail delivery until the first of next week. My road is impassable and the drifts are rising. A neighbor has just knocked at my door to see if I wanted my driveway ploughed, but he can't do it for free.

The price of regular gas just rose another forty cents per gallon, but my car can safely stay in the garage for a couple more days with the hope that the cost of filling the tank will decrease and the snow will be melting by then.

The cupboard and refrigerator are stocked, my Saturday gig has been canceled and why in the world do I even want to go out anyway? The blankets and drifts of snow in my yard actually give me a warm feeling as I watch the flakes get larger, blowing aimlessly in the wind that swirls around my house.

This calls for cuddling up on the sofa with those chocolate and peanut butter chip cookies I discovered at the market. At times like these, who cares about the diet? Where's that bag of potato chips I was hiding from myself?

It's cold, I'm snowed in and the snacks are all mine!

$\mathcal{Y}$ou Have More Time for Yourself

Reason #84

If you're a workaholic like me, it always seems as though you never have time for yourself. I've checked out the time management how-to books and tried to schedule 'me time' on the calendar, but pampering myself rarely happens.

It's an absolute truth that the body, mind and soul need to be fed with peaceful, comforting nourishment. They say that even a half an hour each day helps so much and it can definitely be worked into anyone's busy schedule. Living a single lifestyle affords more opportunities for tranquil time alone and there should be no excuses to skip them. Just think of what you could be doing.

I grew up in the florist business and although the shop is gone, it's a magical feeling when I buy myself a bouquet of flowers that not only feed my senses, but brighten my home and make me smile. The fragrance of roses and hyacinths bring back special memories of my childhood.

The cell phone, answering machine and email have become an addiction in this fast paced world, yet still, everything can wait. You can return calls and messages after your fifteen minutes of meditation. Cozying up with a good book is one of the greatest escapes. *"Take a long walk,"* you say? Yes! Imagine yourself out there on a warm September afternoon with the leaves falling and the scent of autumn in the air! After work, take the long way home. Seek a new route and change of scene.

If you love to dance, make a mix of your favorite songs, turn it up and let yourself go. Make music a part of your life and your soul's nourishment. The powerful, healing properties of frequencies and tones can either be soothing or rev up those good endorphins.

If you're single, who's stopping you from soaking in the bathtub? Stop saving those delightful candles for a special event, light them now!

Is the beach near where you live? Aaah, lucky you! Need I say more?

Serenity, Peace and Quiet

As the lungs are dependent on taking the next breath, the soul demands its independence and the mind thirsts for serenity.

When I think of all of the things that make life easier as a single person, the list is long. I need to be the sole owner of the keys. Maybe some of us have just never found that one companion to live with, like two peas in a pod, but I prefer being human and not a pea.

The older I get, I miss being that child who felt safe and fell asleep on the back seat of the car when my father was at the wheel. Was it simply a matter of trust? It was easy to feel at peace back then.

As a creative spirit, I've discovered that it's nearly impossible to share space with others in the same household. The need for a quiet environment is priority for me in order to focus. If your career is guided by your muse, I know you understand.

You Can Build Your Own Wealth

Reason #82

We're all searching for that pot of gold at the end of the rainbow, whether it provides capital to launch a dream or allows us the freedom to have what we want, while keeping all of the bills paid.

The Internet is filled with empty opportunities and get-rich-quick schemes, but the real principles that build wealth haven't changed for centuries. According to Benjamin Franklin, your journey can begin with reading his book, *"The Way to Wealth"*, where you may find all the wisdom you need to amass a fortune. Granted, it's still going to take hard work, focus, and discipline, but do you have the passion?

Franklin's book is a quick read, just thirty pages filled with financial wisdom. *"The Way to Wealth"* is an essay first published in 1758 as a preface to Franklin's *"Poor Richard's Almanac"*, with seventy-eight maxims, written by our beloved founding father himself.

Here are just a few:
"Early to bed and early to rise makes a man healthy, wealthy and wise"
"Never leave that till tomorrow, which you can do today"
"God helps those who help themselves"
"He that lives upon hope will die fasting"
"There are no gains without pains"

On the importance of saving, Franklin's Father Abraham said, *"If you would be wealthy, think of saving, as well as of getting. Away, then, with your expensive follies, and you will not have then so much reason to complain of hard times."* These words still resonate true today. On the constant need to buy clothes and goods: *"What use is this pride of appearance, for which so much is suffered? It cannot promote health, nor ease pain. It makes no increase of merit in a person, it creates envy, and it hastens misfortune."* Father Abraham then asks, *"What madness must it be to run in debt for these superfluities?"*

I wonder, shouldn't the *"The Way to Wealth"* be required reading at the high school level? Franklin's image is on the U.S. one-hundred dollar bill. His timeless advice is priceless.

*Y*ou Don't Have to Miss Being You

Reason #81

Brenda has been married for nine years now, but has a lot of regrets. The time she spends thinking about the past has taken priority and growing by the day. Because she misses all the friends she never sees anymore, she feels trapped between wanting her former life back and spending precious time with her husband and children.

She loves her family, but doesn't feel like she's the same person she used to be. It stands to reason that responsibilities and transitions in one's life change a person, but Brenda just can't seem to accept the person that she has become. She looks in the mirror and doesn't recognize the person staring back.

Brenda frequently ponders if she likes being a wife and mother. She thinks that it would be nice to be able to go back just for one day and wonders if she would have been happier staying single, where you never miss all the things you used to be able to do before you got married.

You Can Lick the Spoon

Living single has its advantages. Unless you embarrass yourself and feel totally like a slob while drinking directly from the milk jug, it's so much more convenient than taking the time to get a glass from the cupboard. If you must, go for it!

However, certain food items start to look unappetizing with similar liberties. If you take a bite out of a tomato and put it back in the veggie keeper, it's going to get ugly. It may be wise to store less chewed on food.

The love affair between a cook and his or her precious time in the kitchen has a completely different set of rules if you're cooking for one. What gourmet cook doesn't experiment and check the flavor of sauces and broths during meal preparation? There's no need to keep using a clean spoon, then another one and another one.

Who can argue with the pleasure gained from baking cakes? After the batter is poured into the cake pans, the real fun begins. Just please be sure to disconnect the power to the mixer before licking the beaters!

"He is his own best friend, and takes delight in privacy whereas the man of no virtue or ability is his own worst enemy and is afraid of solitude."

. . . Aristotle

No One Changes the Settings on Your Car Radio Or iPod

Reason #79

Before we all had personal iPods and satellite radio, it was a pain to get into the car and find that the other person who owns the spare set of keys had re-programmed all the channels.

Gina is tired of someone invading her space. New car stereos are complicated enough to program, but she isn't the kind of person that likes reading the manual. Arguments and debates over the TV channels or radio settings have thrown a wrench into too many days for her.

Gina lives with her sister Jozzy, who one morning decided to paint their apartment and surprise Gina. Joz wanted to play some tunes while she was working and downloaded new music to Gina's iPod. She had never done it before, but figured it would be easy enough. Unfortunately, something went wrong in the process and she ended up deleting what Gina had stored over many months.

Gina arrived home to a freshly painted living room, but went from being grateful to angry when she discovered that she would have to perform a full software restore to her iPod, after her sister lost hundreds of songs that had been stored.

$\mathcal{Y}$ou Can Primp for Hours

Reason #78

If you have a hot date coming up or just want to pamper yourself, you have the freedom to indulge whenever you like.

Get a manicure, pedicure, a massage. If you've ever dreamed of having an entire day of going through your wardrobe and weeding out what you don't wear anymore, here's your chance. You don't have to wait for a rainy day.

Spend the day at a spa or get your hair weaved. Try a new hairstyle. Re-invent yourself.

Here's a refreshing mask that will give your face a new glow:

"Green Apple and Yogurt Mask"

Peel one green apple
Place one quarter of the apple into blender
Add 2 tablespoons of honey and 2 ounces of plain yogurt
Blend together in a blender until a smooth paste is formed

Refrigerate for 2 hours

Apply gently and leave on face for 10 minutes
Rinse with warm water

$\mathcal{Y}$ou Can Keep Your Maiden Name

Reason #77

For a single woman, it's so simple and sweet to keep your maiden name. A few years ago, I came across an article covering an in-depth study on women suffering from identity crisis, stemming from taking their spouse's name. It stated that the psychological effects on some women can evolve into a crisis, where they actually begin to feel that they don't even know who they are anymore. This remains a critical issue for many women today.

Women who have chosen to take their husband's name can range from those who don't really see it as an issue to those who fear that if they don't, their children's identity will be lost or confused. Those who have elected to keep their given names see there are several advantages. Some believe in the importance of carrying on the identity of their lineage; others simply love their name, have had it all their lives and wouldn't change it for any reason; and there are those who don't want the hassle of the legal red tape, which can get even more complicated if a woman divorces and wants her maiden name back.

For the past several decades, legally changing their names has further complicated the lives of many divorced women. Taking back their maiden name left them non-existent, alienated in a world that used to know them as Mrs. Someone, leaving them as Ms. No One with zero credit history. Whether you're changing your name back to your own or taking his, there are still challenges.

Let's make a list: A new driver's license, passport, social security card, checking account, savings account, 401k plan, stocks, certificates, bonds or mutual funds, credit cards, subscriptions, membership cards, wills, mortgages, car loans, medical records, insurance policies, living will, any legal documents and on and on.

Barbara in Texas says, *"I didn't change my last name when I married, partly because my law license and diplomas bear my maiden name, but also because I didn't feel like changing or discarding the name given to me at birth."*

Tom from Oregon says, *"Whenever my wife calls someplace regarding the kids (doctors, daycare, etc.), she has to say, 'This is Jane Smith, John Doe's mother.' Me, I can simply say, 'This is Tom Doe, John's father.' I've had problems picking up prescriptions for my wife when she can't because of our different names. My wife also carries a copy of our marriage license on her at all times."*

Angie in North Carolina says, *"The best solution I came across was a couple that picked a brand new last name for themselves. I have three sets of friends who did this!"*

Julia in Chicago says, *"I've seen a lot of variations in my time as a professor, and my current Dean has a hyphenated name, (but his wife does not!). I've talked about it with my partner and she, like me, shares the publishing dilemma concern."*

Which leads us to yet another name issue- to hyphenate or not to hyphenate. When we heard that our former First Lady, also Senator from the State of New York and currently the U.S. Secretary of State had officially changed her name to Hillary Rodham Clinton, it raised the validation level for many married women. I'm sure old Lucy Stone would have had plenty to say about that.

One century ago, Lucy waged a passionate struggle for equal rights for women, a struggle that continues even in today's world. In existence since the early 1920's, The Lucy Stone League is dedicated to equal rights for women and men to retain, modify and create their own names, believing that a person's name is fundamental to his or her existence.

According to a study by Harvard economics professor Claudia Goldin, based on Massachusetts birth records, the number of college-educated women in their thirties who have kept their given name, dropped from 23 percent in 1990 to 17 percent in 2000. Those traveling the traditional route by taking his name, join the ranks of 90 percent of women getting married today in the United States.

So . . . single? Wasn't it great to wake up this morning without having to deal with all of that mumbo-jumbo? Isn't it wonderful to know who you truly are?

$\mathcal{Y}$ou Can Decorate and Place the Furniture Wherever You Want

I met my second husband at a local radio station where we both worked on the air. He was AM and I was FM, exchanging glances through the studio windows.

To say that I was shocked when I first visited his apartment is quite an understatement. I'll spare you the details. I had never been inside someone's bachelor pad before and learned to appreciate that my first husband never lived like a cave man. At this point, I had been divorced for a few years and in the process of building my second house. We decided to live together, but now that I look back, I wasn't ready to share my dream home with Java Man.

The day he moved in, I learned a lot about myself. As each box and 'man thing' was carried into what would no longer be just my space, I cringed. *"Was I already set in my ways, too eccentric, too feminine with my décor?"* I thought. *"Would I have the interior design skills to blend my Country French furnishings with his 1960's rattan patio group that still possessed the musty odor of his parent's basement?"*

My second ex is a Beatles fan and collector of Beatle's music and memorabilia. However, his life-sized poster of the band from the "Introducing the Beatles" album cover became a challenge for me. Me, who also loved the fab four since childhood, inspiring my songwriting skills and musical tastes. At eleven years of age, I actually believed that I would marry Paul McCartney as soon as he dumped Jane Asher, but Linda Eastman beat me to it!

At twenty-eight, I had missed my chance with Mr. McCartney and married Java Man. There stood Paul staring back at me from my living room wall. How would I break it to my husband that his beloved Beatle's poster, under glass in its sturdy brass frame, was more apropos for a college dorm? Paul, George, John and Ringo eventually found a home downstairs in the recreation room with the moldy rattan furniture.

Years after we parted, he emailed to let me know that accidentally, the poster fell and the glass shattered. I sometimes wonder if the poster would be cool hanging in my music studio today. Have I changed? Could I really be that tolerant now?

I do feel fortunate that my ex was a Beatle's fan and not a beer can collector. Even Dodi Fayed had a huge wall covered with his ball cap collection. Hmmmmm, I wonder what Princess Diana thought of Dodi's Paris bachelor pad?

If you're still on the fence about staying single, take your time and be observant. When he moves in and wants to display his little plastic army soldiers on the window sill, run as fast as you can!

Freedom to Pursue Your Passion

What is your passion? Maybe it's gourmet cooking, golf, flying, building canoes or carving totem poles. Your passion can be your life's work or a hobby that you love. I'm not saying that you cannot pursue your passion if you were married or in a relationship, but it's less stressful when you're single.

As a writer, I can attest to countless sleepless nights and long days that take my attention away from anything else but writing. In many situations, it's difficult for others to understand, but when the creative juices start to flow, I must follow. It isn't easy to just hang out now and then with family and friends.

At times, the dog or the cats refuse to understand and they demand my immediate attention. In fact, at this very moment, I've had to stop and break up a cat fight in the basement.

Personally, I've been far more successful during the periods of my life when I have been on my own. Reaching the summit of your full potential is still a tough climb, but far less complicated when a spouse or partner isn't trying to drag you back down the mountain.

No Drama

Aaah, listen! Do you hear that? Exactly. Peace and quiet, (unless you're reading this book on the subway right now).

No one else is kicking up the dust in your sacred sanctuary, the dust being a debate or disagreement about something as meaningless as the toothpaste cap that has turned up missing. Do you co-habitate with someone like this?

If you do, excuse me for being cliché, but life is too short. Why do we waste so much time and effort in heated discussions over spilt milk? If the toast burns, turn down the toaster dial and put in another slice. Move on and be free with your righteous piece of toast and throw the burnt one outside for the little sparrows. They're hungry.

Most of the time, the drama queen or king you're living with needs way more attention than you can give them. If you live in a metropolitan city and want drama, you can go out on the balcony of your apartment and yell, *"Go away and leave me alone!"*

Actually, you may not want to do that because in some neighborhoods, someone will yell back!

*Y*ou Can Have As Many Sleeping Partners As You Like

If you are so inclined, you can see a different face on the pillow next to you every morning, any day of the week.

Sean admits that his lifestyle is one where he enjoys seeing different women. He has many friends who are women and several have the potential of becoming a steady girlfriend. If that were the case, however, he'd have to sacrifice the wonderful relationships he has with the other women in his life.

A few of these relationships have become intimate. Once he realized that there was a different woman in his bed four or five times per week, he felt a little guilty, but it's his business and it works for Sean at this stage in his life. That isn't a standard he's set for himself, it has just happened.

Living single brings more opportunities to meet new people and wherever it leads is in the hands of fate. One day Sean may find the woman who he wants to spend the rest of his life with. For now, life is fun and exciting with no strings attached.

What did you say your name was?

$\mathscr{L}$ucy, There's No S'Plainin' to Do

When Paula was living under her parent's roof, she showed them respect, didn't come home at all hours of the night and proved to be the responsible, considerate person they taught her to be.

When she was finally moved out on her own, she answered to only herself. Her mom and dad have always been so cool when it comes to respecting her privacy, but her freedom suddenly changed when she took in a roommate who eventually became her boyfriend.

Paula is a graphics designer by trade and there are many nights that call for working late to meet certain deadlines. At first, her boyfriend Greg was okay with it. Now she feels that she has to go through an inquisition when she comes through the door. If Greg is asleep when she gets home, he fires up the Q. & A. over breakfast.

Now, she misses being single and having the luxury of being independent and never having to explain about what she's doing and where she's been, especially when she has nothing to hide. Unless he can change, the days of living with Greg are numbered.

There Is More to Life after the Loss of a Spouse

Reason #71

Tracey misses her husband and the life they had together, but she knows that a new door has opened for her and her late husband would want her to live life at the fullest. He would have known that he had her blessing to do the same if she had gone before him.

When they first received the diagnosis that Gill had cancer, they both believed that he could beat it. Gill was one of those guys who was athletic and strong, as if he'd live forever. He was willing to do whatever it took to cleanse his body from the cancer cells, whether it was the poison they pumped through his veins or herbal remedies that claimed to be a cure.

The night he passed away, their son was there by Gill's side. Tracey had stepped out for a few minutes to go to the chapel and when she returned to his room, Gill was gone. She believes that he wanted to slip away quickly so she wouldn't have to witness it. He always protected her like that. Their son told her they had prayed together as he helped his dad hold his rosary.

For five years, Tracey lived with guilt and anxiety, feeling that she had failed at protecting or saving Gill. One night she dreamt about him, as he whispered something to her that didn't make sense at first. He said, *"It's your turn to heal."*

She finally decided to volunteer for a local cancer support group where her life began to change dramatically. Her days are now filled with making new friends she would have never had and witnessing amazing miracles.

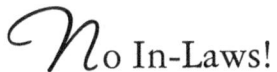

No In-Laws!

I grew up in the Catholic faith, following in my father's footsteps, under the dominant rule of the Dominican nuns and priests. Along with my school mates, I attended Mass every Wednesday morning before school and occasional Sundays with my dad.

The years of teachings from the catechism were troubling, but I was fearful of asking questions or debating issues that never seemed to make any sense. The day of my First Communion was the first important event of my life. Everyone was dressed in white and our photos were taken standing in front of the statue of the Blessed Virgin in the courtyard of the church. It was a warm day in May and my mother looked so pretty in her floral suit and matching hat. I could sense her angst, feeling uncomfortable with the members of the church.

My mother was a Methodist. She still tells the story to this day of how the priest forced her to sign a document stating that every child born in her marriage to my father would exclusively be raised as a Catholic. I witnessed the cultural differences within my family and learned quickly how polarizing each religious belief could be. My grandparents on either side of the family never gelled and I observed the discord with the dreaded 'mothers-in-law'.

Continually, I experienced the prejudiced attitude of the nuns and how they acted out their feelings on the children of mixed marriages. I became increasingly uncomfortable in class, when the nuns, who were also the elementary teachers, would ask the students the same questions repeatedly throughout grade school: *"How many girls are planning to become a nun when they grow up?"* and *"How many boys are planning to become a priest?"* In the clusters of raised hands, I never participated with a reply.

As a young adult, I was uncertain of what I truly believed in and practiced a lot of soul searching about God and Jesus Christ. After several years of personal study of Buddhism, Christianity and Judaism, I discovered that the Jewish faith came closer to my beliefs and finally found comfort in my own relationship with God.

In my late twenties, I met a man who was Jewish, whose family were members of a conservative temple. I fell in love with him, but he struggled with the fear of having to break it to his parents that he had met a non-Jew and was considering marriage. He had dated several Gentile girls, but never told his parents about them. His mother was compassionate, understanding and always a pleasure to be with. However, when I shook my future father-in-law's hand for the first time, he looked me straight in the eye and firmly stated, *"I don't like convertibles!"*

Forging on, I converted into the Jewish faith and married who I believed was the man of my dreams, but never won the hearts of my in-laws. It is my firm belief that they patiently waited along the sidelines for the marriage to fail, which it did after five alienating years. Since then, I have never remarried. My ex later re-married a Jewish woman, satisfying the will of his father and finally making peace in the family.

Millions have found love and lasting relationships in mixed marriages. Their successes are forged from families who are more culturally objective and comfortable with who they are themselves. In our marriage, religious tradition held power over love and acceptance. Parents, who indulge in impressing their friends and colleagues, force their children to exist behind a veil of prejudice. In-laws? They can make or break a marriage.

"I never found a companion that was so companionable as solitude."

. . . Henry David Thoreau

*Y*ou Don't Have to Share Anything with Anyone

Reason #69

Jamie is one of seven kids in her family. She believes that her selfishness is due to growing up in a house where nothing seemed to belong to only her. Whether it was clothing, shoes, toys, a toothbrush, even eating utensils, it was shared and no one thought a thing about it.

When she moved out and found a place of her own, she vowed that everything she possessed was sacred. One of Jamie's friends has moved into an apartment recently, but has a roommate who asks to borrow clothes constantly. A pair of her good shoes is now missing and she's freaking out about what to do with her valuables or loose cash. Should Jamie's friend get a new roommate? Probably, but it won't be Jamie. She's just getting cozy and living happily on her own.

Jamie admits that when her brothers stop by for a visit, she gets nervous when they begin to appear to be too comfortable. She just wants to tell them that she's busy and to be on their merry way. *"It sounds mean,"* she says, *"but I want some peace and quiet, my OWN space and all the fingerprints are mine!"*

*V*ibrators Don't Talk Back

"Who said that women can't have orgasms too?" Haley asks. Her boyfriend has set certain standards with regard to their lovemaking. *"I don't make the rules,"* she says, *"but my boyfriend believes that he does."*

When it comes to sex, if Haley can't keep up with her boyfriend, it's too bad for her. He says that it's an insult to him if she's not turned on enough to have an orgasm along with him. She wonders what you do with someone who practically ejaculates at lightning speed.

The last straw was the day he called her at work and told her to meet him at home for lunch. When she got there, he was waiting for her in their bedroom. They made love in less than five minutes. He suddenly jumped up, raced into the shower and dressed, announcing he had to go because he had a meeting. Haley stared at the ceiling, feeling abandoned on the wet sheets. Angry and messy, she decided that she was finished tolerating his condescending attitude.

She's moving out soon, cannot wait to have her own place and dump all of the anxiety she's had with this guy. Since he thinks he has to have the final word, he has told her that now she can pleasure herself with a vibrator and how much she's going to miss having sex with him.

By any means, Haley won't miss his tiny penis. Her answer to him is, *"At least vibrators aren't pompous bastards and they don't talk back."*

You Can Choose to Flush . . . Or Not

Once upon a time, Jeremy was living in a little apartment in lower Manhattan that was no bigger than the kitchen of the house he lives in today. The rent for the apartment was enormous and the water bill was highway robbery. He did everything to save water and use as little as he possibly could. Conserving water for drinking, the shower, washing dishes, and cooking was a challenge.

That's when he became accustomed to not flushing the toilet at night. Who was going to know? It's embarrassing for him to admit, but that habit developed into not flushing during the day until he was sure he wasn't going to overflow the bowl. If it started to smell too bad, he just opened a window.

As long as he didn't have company, it was cool and he was saving big time on his water bill. The neighbors on his floor never complained. The odors coming from their places were gross enough. Maybe they weren't flushing their toilets either. Who knows?

Jeremy's income is greater today and his water bill is actually lower. His advice is that when you're single, you can choose to flush or not, but he really doesn't recommend it!

You Don't Have to Make Excuses for Your Behavior

Reason #66

Anthony lived with a girl who had to know everything and why. She was relentless, always asking him *"What are you thinking right now this minute?"* or *"Why do you have to chew so loud?"*

If he wanted to hang out with the guys, she had to know who he was going to be with, as if his college buddies were going to lead him astray or get him into trouble. She didn't trust him at all and had no reason not to. Anthony was apologizing for things he didn't even do.

If he went to the refrigerator to get a soda, she'd tell him to stay out of the kitchen because she'd just cleaned. He had a favorite pair of sneakers that she hated to the point that he felt guilty when he wore them. Believe it or not, she didn't throw them away.

Anthony claims that before you know it, you're telling lies, hiding stuff and making excuses for meaningless crap. His former girlfriend pushed him to the point where he was paranoid about anything he did or said when he was in her company. Her royal highness is long gone now. It's just Anthony, his dog and his own thoughts and habits.

*Y*ou Can Be Messy and Leave It That Way
Reason #65

Some prefer to stay single because they just don't make a great housemate, no matter how hard they try.

Dane has had a few girlfriends and even male roommates. Over the years, he's been called a pig, a troll, a worthless, no good, lazy, %$@&*())(&@! and more. Being a messy person even bothers Dane himself. It's not just girlfriends, lovers and roommates, but his accountant isn't very happy with him either, especially at tax time.

Of course, Dane isn't the only person in the world born without the clean gene. I guess you could say that being single is the easiest form of existence for him because he can leave everything as he pleases and never suffers through the rants about how the place looks like a hurricane just struck. At work, his secretary loses it when his desk gets piled up with paperwork, but somehow he actually knows where everything is.

Life for men like Dane can be a little dangerous, as one of his closets is like something you'd see on a TV sit com. When you open the door, a million things fall out and hit you on the head. Ten pound hand weights are not good stored up above on a shelf!

So, you can call him anything you like. That's Dane, that's what you get and it will all be organized in some fashion someday.

You Can Focus On Your Own Schedule
Reason #64

Have you looked at your calendar lately?

If you're a single parent, this certainly does not apply to you. You deserve applause . . . no . . . a standing ovation and congratulations for your efforts of juggling kids, school, household chores and your own career. You are the shining example of how to be a champion at staying focused while being challenged by constant interruption.

How many of us have to check someone else's schedule before we can schedule a dental appointment or an oil change? I have a friend who carried around a pocket calendar in her bag for years. She had to list what she was doing, what her husband was doing, her daughter's activities and more. Her handwriting had to be so tiny to squeeze it all into each square of each month, I don't know how she kept it all straight. She has a blackberry now, but still has to enter everyone's info and juggle the entire family's events.

Men seem to be able to feel less stressed over this issue when compared to women. Some guys can take a lunch break and get a quick haircut and be back at work without being missed.

If you're fortunate to have just your own life to focus on, don't get too cozy yet. There are birthdays and other events to always remember.

*Y*ou're Not Desperate to Find a Mate

Reason #63

"So why haven't you gotten married again?" If I had a dollar for every time I have been asked that question, I would . . . well, you know what I mean.

Single men and women are not lonely and desperate by any means. You are not half of a person if you're no longer half of a couple. I ask, *"Why should I give up my independence and my privacy again?"*

Instead of looking for a mate, singles are now looking for power and control of their own destiny. Being single will make you stronger, give you focus, allow you to indulge in the simple pleasures of life, teach you self-love and the ability to appreciate yourself with or without a mate. Many single women now focus on building a life of their own, rather than counting on a man to provide it for them.

It has been said that singles are *"a potentially powerful socio-economic group, but one that is still widely perceived as disadvantaged or insignificant, subordinate or invisible."* At times, our society has portrayed single people as washed up spinsters and/or confirmed bachelors, but in spite of the pressures of our culture, millions of singles are embracing life, however they desire, with almost unlimited independence. What could be better than that?

The Shower Is All Yours

Here are the top five reasons to celebrate having your own bathtub:

1. There is no one else in the house waiting to take a shower and worrying about whether there will be enough hot water for them.

2. You can steam up the mirror and not interfere with someone who is using the sink or vanity at the same time.

3. No one is going to flush the toilet and change the temperature of the water while you're right in the middle of rinsing your face!

4. You can relax and be rest assured that your towel will still be hanging there when you're ready to get out of the shower.

5. If you don't have to worry about conserving water, you can turn on the shower and let it warm up for a few minutes before you get in.

These are just a few little luxuries of the steamy single life!

$\mathcal{U}$ndisturbed Sleep

How does this sound to you- an entire night of undisturbed sleep?

No one else is watching television, snoring, coughing, sneezing or making noise from the next room. The bed, the sheets, the pillows, the comforter, the blankets, the lamp, the night stand, the bedroom is all yours.

If you prefer, you can keep the television on all night, even while you're sleeping. For some it helps them to doze off. If you need a night-light, it's yours and doesn't bother anyone else who has to have total darkness for a solid night's sleep.

Maybe you like to sleep with the windows cracked open in the middle of winter and you tuck in under three poufy comforters. If the air conditioner is too cold for your own comfort in the summer months, YOU can shut it off.

. . . By the way, you are the master of the thermostat!

Nighty-night.

Shhhhhhhhhhhh!

*Y*ou Can Go to Bed Whenever You Like

Reason #60

If you're one to burn the midnight oil like me, this issue comes up frequently when your spouse or lover wants you to go to bed when they do. You might have just one more little thing you have to do, get a glass of water or *"I'm almost finished with this article and I'll be up soon,"* you say.

Whether I'm writing a song, catching up on email or entering the day's events in my journal, there are nights that seem to call out to me. When you're single, you can keep going till breakfast and sleep when you're sleepy.

The bigger question is, *"Why should someone get upset with you when you need some time for yourself and maybe that time works best for you in the middle of the night?"* You may wonder why, if someone really loves you, they don't give you the freedom to spend your time the way you like during the day, night or all night.

Maybe they are hoping to get a night of undisturbed sleep for themselves!

"He who knows others is wise. He who knows himself is enlightened."

. . . Lao Tzu

You Can Come and Go as You Please

"Come and go as you please."

The mere sight or sound of those words just make you feel good. And who's stopping you? Why not enjoy life and its simplest of pleasures without restrictions? There is no need to clock in and out, announce when you'll return or explain where you've been.

Picture this: you have a garden of flowers and vegetables. It's one of the greatest escapes you've ever known and the pride you have about growing your favorite plants grows with them. Just think of the money you're saving and how much better those tomatoes taste right out of your own back yard. You're digging and weeding one afternoon and hear the phone ring from the house. No one is calling to you that you have to go in and answer it or that someone is waiting to talk to you. You let the voicemail capture it and enjoy the smell of the earth on your hands. Please don't remind me that you can take your cell phone to the garden with you. Escape for just once!

As stressful and complicated as life has become, you can still take control and find a way to live more freely. Living single could possibly help to make that happen. Whatever road you choose, be sure to have your day in the sun!

*Y*ou Can Surf the Internet with Privacy

Gwen's former boyfriend Ted is a computer geek. He takes care of making sure his laptop and other computers don't get corrupted. Twice a week, he cleans out the cache and anything he doesn't want to save in the temporary Internet files.

When they moved in together, he asked if she'd like for him to maintain her laptop and she thought it was a great idea. It was one more thing she didn't have to worry about, only it evolved into something that became a new problem.

If she had been surfing around looking at sites about her favorite celebs or cute looking guys, Ted would question about what she had been looking at online. It wasn't like Gwen was downloading porn, which she's certain he did, especially since he could clean out anything he had viewed immediately.

Single 101 blogs are a perfect example of Gwen's dilemma. Some readers are uncomfortable with leaving a comment because people like Ted would find it and ask why their lover or spouse was reading about being single, as if that would threaten their relationship.

Is nothing sacred when you're involved with someone, whether you're married or just living together?

You Don't Have to Be in a Relationship To Feel Complete

It's all about the power of individuality. How easy it is to lose yourself in someone because you love them so much and tragic when you allow your own identity to disappear.

Some people feel that they actually need to be attached to someone to look and feel better about themselves, similar to women who believe that they must have children to feel complete.

Many women feel more content and at ease living with a man or partner that offers a sense of security and safety, but my cat is a better guardian angel than several of my former boyfriends.

I heard a recently divorced woman say that now she is single in a married world. It's not a married or coupled world at all, only how you choose to perceive it. There are many fairytales out there, but you do not have to be in a relationship to live happily ever after.

*Y*ou Can Have A Party Anytime

Wouldn't it be fun to call your friends at the spur of the moment and announce you're having a party tonight? You don't have to ask for permission or check to see if it's okay with your roommate or spouse. How much fun would that be to throw a party whenever you wanted and serve whatever you know your friends would love?

Impromptu dinner parties help when the fridge is almost bare as well. In troubled economic times, getting creative helps to survive. Host a 'Chili Night' in the middle of winter. Request that each person bring a different ingredient for a big pot of chili, B.Y.O.B., a loaf of crusty bread and you're all set. Be good to the environment and use real plates, bowls, glasses and tableware, even cloth napkins to dress up your event. Someone may even stay to help with the dishes.

If you have a group of friends who are also single, take turns hosting a 'Flying Solo Party'. I guarantee you'll have many evenings of memorable conversation and laughter.

$\mathcal{Y}$ou Can Work Out or Diet Because You Want To

Brooke felt pressured by her husband that her hips and thighs were too big. No matter what diet she tried, she lost inches everywhere else but in the right places. She joined a gym to get help from a personal trainer, knowing there was a lot more to learn about diet and exercise and prayed that it would please her husband.

In just a few months, she worked a couple of inches off of her hips, but it wasn't enough to convince her that the gym membership was making that big of a difference. The stress from her husband's ridicule made her feel like such a failure. Brooke finally moved out and got her own place.

After a year had gone by, she'd lost five inches off of her hips and two inches off each thigh. Her goals were now about what she wanted, not what her husband needed her to be. She discovered that without his criticism and with total encouragement from friends and other members at the gym, she found success.

Brooke and her husband are only separated, but their divorce will be final soon. He has noticed that she lost weight, but she is not going to stay with him if that's why he shows interest in her again. Another relationship or marriage in the future isn't a priority for her, just her own happiness, pride and self-respect.

*Y*ou Can Keep Your Toys

According to Pat, the single life provides many freedoms, especially when it comes to your precious possessions.

Pat was married for four years and then lived with another woman briefly, but neither of them were crazy about his Harley, sports gear or bass guitar. In both situations, he grew tired of the nagging. Both of these gals thought that if he didn't use something often enough, it wasn't worth keeping.

Pat believes that he's a decent guy, clean and organized. It wasn't like he was parking his hog in the bedroom, but he knows guys who do. His baseball gear has its own space in the closet and he likes to have his bass sitting on its stand in the living room. It's an expensive instrument and a joy to own. He loves to play blues and very proud to display his guitar.

No matter what he did to try to be out of someone's way, it wasn't good enough. Now, he's free and loving what single life brings.

You Never Have to Hide Items in Your Shopping Cart

Reason #53

Brandon claims that his girlfriend is the commandant of the food budget police. He claims that when they shop at the grocery, which she insists on doing together, she turns into this 'watch how it's done' monster.

She has to exhibit how to look for bargains, read labels and to pay attention to the salt and cholesterol levels. It's so extreme, that going to the grocery store has become a part of life that he absolutely detests. Anxiety sets in when it's time to go shopping and Brandon has lost his appetite.

If he tries to hide a bag of chips or cookies in the cart, her radar picks it up immediately and back onto the shelf they go. Recently, she's been reading about how certain foods shouldn't be mixed together or how they should completely delete wheat from their diets.

She says it's not in their budget for a magazine or video. Brandon's girlfriend means well. He loves her, but she is no fun whatsoever. Brandon wishes he was single again and would never have to feel like he committed a crime if he hides the cheese!

No Curfew

Reason #52

Taylor thought that curfews were over when she moved out of her parent's house. Her roommate Kelley thinks they should both have a curfew and not stay out late. One morning, Kelley sarcastically asked Taylor why she just didn't stay out all night, if she was going to be so late coming home.

Since they share the rent and utilities, split household chores and even take turns cooking, Taylor feels that she has the right to do whatever she likes on her own time. When she's out on a date and comes home in the wee hours of the morning, she's always quiet and considerate not to make any noise and wake up Kelley.

Taylor wonders if the next thing will be a complaint about her cat. Will she have to be sure that she cleans the litter box before midnight? Then, what's next after that?

Unfortunately for both, Kelley is either turning into a mother hen or becoming too nosy about Taylor's business. Taylor has not realized that she still has to make some sacrifices if she's rooming with someone, although she is just one step away from the freedom she's looking for.

So, until she can afford a new place all her own or find another roommate who shares the same kind of lifestyle, Taylor will have to meet Kelley in the middle.

You Never Have To Trade in Miniskirts for Minivans

Reason #51

Ryan has been single since college and he's still not ready to settle down. Life is full of adventure and opportunity right now. Several girls he's dated have attempted maneuvers to get him to commit, but he's been successful so far at staying focused on his engineering career and planning for the future.

One of his friends who got married right after graduating from college says that he regrets making that move so early in life. His advice to Ryan is not to trade his interest in miniskirts for minivans. Not that Ryan has a different girlfriend every week, but he's not ready to give up his space and start changing diapers.

Staying single until he's ready for marriage is the right situation for him now. Ryan would rather stay a bachelor until he reaches his forties and marry only once and for life. Too many of his buddies have taken the plunge and now they're going through the heartache of divorce.

Fortunately for Ryan, there is no pressure from his parents to make them grandparents.

If There's Dribble on Your Pillow, You Know Where It Came From

Reason #50

You know that you are really content living alone when you awaken in the middle of the night with one side of your face all wet, you dry off with the sleeve of your pajama top, turn the pillow over and go back to sleep. If there's dribble on your pillow, you know where it came from.

Doctors will tell you that you can cure this easily, just breathing through your nose and not your mouth. But, how can you control that if you're asleep? They also say to get accustomed to sleeping on your back instead of on one side, claiming that on your back, it is virtually impossible to drool while you're sleeping.

The dribble on my pillow can be inconvenient, but nothing compared to a hot flash at 3:00am. Could it be possible that we drool while dreaming about Mr. Right or buying that vintage Jaguar?

Whatever position you sleep in, thank goodness it's your saliva, unless you sleep with an eighty-five pound slobbering mastiff.

Single 101 Crossword Puzzle

Single 101 Puzzle Clues:

Across

1. The power to endure
7. Being full of life
8. The freedom to be who you are
11. The ability to live life as you choose
12. To make easier
13. To develop and expand
14. Outstanding or superior,
    denoting to one
16. To realize a goal
21. To risk or attempt
22. A feeling of complete happiness
24. To journey any distance
26. To have a strong affection for
    someone or something
27. To wish
29. A state of peace and tranquility
30. Honor with festive ceremonies
31. Amusement and enjoyment
34. To develop or change by degree
35. Unmarried or not involved in
    a relationship
36. Having the liberty to live
    as you choose

Down

2. Change oneself into an improved
   or different state
3. A facial expression of happiness
4. To construct or develop
5. Pleasurable rest
6. Change into a new and different
   way of being
7. Quality that distinguishes a vital
   and functional being
9. Celebrate with great joy
10. Essential person distinct from others
11. To better oneself
14. The act of doing something on the
    spur of the moment
15. State of being simple or less for
    the better
17. Complete feeling of joy
18. To exist
19. A state of total peace and quiet
20. Finding something new and amazing
23. Expression of celebration during
    a toast
25. Measurement of the passing hours,
    days or years
28. To discover and expand one's knowledge
30. The ability to conquer with fortitude
32. To formulate and grow
33. To feel joy outwardly

"When we are unable to find tranquility within ourselves, it is useless to seek it elsewhere."
. . . Francois de la Rochefoucauld

So What if It's Your Period!

Here are the top ten reasons why it's easier to be single during that time of the month:

1. You can use pads or tampons, whatever you like, who cares?

2. You're free to sleep in ratty old panties, no one sees you.

3. You can toss the used pads in the bathroom basket at night and transfer them to the garbage bag later.

4. You are the owner of the heating pad.

5. You never have to send your boyfriend to the drugstore for items that might embarrass him.

6. No one has to hear you whimper and moan when you're having cramps.

7. No one puts pressure on you about when you can have sex again.

8. You never have to discover that you've just started your period during sex.

9. No one else will sneak into the medicine cabinet and steal your Motrin.

10. There are never any sudden movements in your bed from a body lying next to you.

You Can Be a Total Chick Magnet

Reason #48

Living single for Tory means a free and easy lifestyle, especially in the summer, when the hot girls are everywhere. At the beach or in the pubs, everyone is casual, looking cool in their shades. The girls are soaking up the sun in their skimpy bikinis and Tory reminds his buddies that the view is the best in the world.

Since high school, girls have been attracted to him. If he surrenders to just one relationship, he feels stuck. He's made a lot of girls angry, but they finally get over it and find someone else. Tory is one of those guys you read about in chick magazines- the ones who won't commit. He believes that men want to play the field and take their time. No one can argue with that.

Tory feels that it's not as easy as it seems. You have to work at being a chick magnet. The right car, clothes, haircut, the whole package has to be complete. When it comes to hair, he knows the day will come when he's growing less and less of it. Someday, his chick magnet days will be drawing to a close, but he'll ride this wave as long as he can.

What You're Wearing Is Up to You

"You're not going to wear that, are you?"

As if it wasn't enough after years of being interrogated by your mother, there should be a house rule that roommates, lovers and spouses stay out of your business about your wardrobe. If they persist at being a pest about this subject, they need to get their own makeover show.

Comfy jeans and a sweatshirt to go to the grocery are fine with most people. If I'm dressing for a meeting, a performance, a fancy party or night out, there's always going to be an issue with my hair, but I don't need to be judged about what I'm wearing before I go out the door.

I've already changed into seven different outfits on my own!

There's Plenty of Space in the Closet

Reason #46

You can renovate, re-organize or give away the clothes you don't wear anymore and still not have enough room in your closet. According to many single women, it's a beautiful thing to have the space all to yourself.

Madeline is fed up with her husband's stinking running shoes on the floor of the closet, beneath her best gowns and party dresses. She complained about it once. Thinking he would fix the problem, he sprayed deodorant on his shoes. Now her gowns smell worse than the men's locker room.

Natalie can't open the bedroom closet door without being hit in the head by her boyfriend's basketball. She keeps moving it to the garage and it continues to turn up again and again in the closet.

Karen can't believe she's let it get to the point where it's now a battle over his stuff and her stuff. Someone get the measuring tape and the chalk line!

Closet organizing, maximizing space, designer walk-in closets, even stackable baskets can cost more than you think. If you're still searching for a solution for what to do with his stuff, have a yard sale.

You Don't Have to Deal with Someone Else's Mood Swings

Fed up with her husband's mood swings, Miranda struggles with tolerating mediocrity. Every weekend, her husband camps on the couch and only leaves his faithfully guarded spot to either walk to the refrigerator or the bathroom. He hangs out in a tee shirt and work out pants and skips taking a shower. When she asks him if he'd like to clean up, change and go do something with her, he says that he doesn't feel like it. In fact, he doesn't answer right away. He makes a weird face and shrugs his shoulders, then says that he doesn't feel like it.

She realizes that his job is highly stressful and he just wants to shut down for the entire weekend. Throughout the week, he comes home late, sometimes missing dinner. The weeks and months of this behavior have stretched too far and she knows he is definitely in no mood to be with her. If one of his buddies happens to call, he flies off the couch, jumps into the shower and makes sure he's not late to meet with them.

For a while, Miranda pretended to be moody and quiet as well to see how he'd react, but it didn't affect him at all. He was too busy working hard at being a sourpuss. Her husband refuses to go to counseling with her, leaving them in a foggy co-existence.

Miranda has decided to go on with her life and let the cards fall where they may.

You Don't Fret Over Bathroom Odors

"You never have to worry about what your bathroom smells like when you've finished using it."

Alecia remembers when her dad used to read the newspaper in the bathroom. Her mom would say to him, *"Flush it, will ya?"* and *"Do you have to camp in there?"* When he would finally come out of the 'library', as he referred to it, he would joke and say that his shit didn't stink and smelled like chocolate. The family would all roll their eyes and laugh along with him.

Linda claims that she really lived with Pepe LePew for a few months. Unfortunately for her, they shared the same bathroom. One night he came home after having way too many hot dogs and beers at the game. There were remnants of the stadium concession stand all over the sink, mirror and commode. Mr. LePew was too sick to clean it up himself. Linda went next door to ask her neighbor if she could use their bathroom.

So, light a match or spray potpourri if you need to, just in case someone is at the door and has stopped by for a surprise visit.

You Can Sleep in or Take Naps Whenever You Like

Reason #43

Kay lives on Staten Island and works in New York City. For several years she was single and loved it. When the economy fell apart, she had to take in a roommate to help with the rent and expenses. When she screened potential roomies, she made sure that the person would be compatible with her schedule and lifestyle, but it's not turning out the way she had hoped.

Working in Manhattan is stressful enough. She has to take a ferry and then ride the subway to and from work, dealing with bums, beggars and people that stink. The length of time it cuts into her schedule dictates how early she has to rise each morning and how late she gets home each night. When she does get home, she just wants to crash, eat when she feels like it and taking a nap on a Sunday afternoon would be glorious! Over the past couple of years that she's lived in her building, she's actually been able to fall asleep when the guy next door plays his guitar, but her roommate is a different story.

Her roommate Sandra, (who must never be called Sandy), only answers to 'Sandra'. She is an artist and stays home most of the day working on her paintings or lying around thinking up new ideas for new paintings. Sandra is one of those lucky people who happen to sell a piece of art just in time when the rent is due and flies by the seat of her pants. She's great about keeping her supplies and work area divided off from Kay's living quarters, but she always seems to have an epiphany or new art assignment that necessitates working through the night or all weekend. To add insult to injury, she can't paint unless she's playing her heavy metal tunes. So, the place is rockin' just when Kay is desperate for a good night's sleep.

Kay needs a better job, more money, a new place of her own and some sleep . . . now!

$\mathcal{Y}$ou Can Take a Vacation Anytime and Anywhere

Reason #42

The single life affords one of the greatest luxuries if you have the time and resources. You can take a vacation or get away for a weekend anytime you like and go anywhere you want without compromise. When vacation time is here, who's stopping you? There isn't anyone you have to please or compromise with when it comes to where you'd like to go. You can stay where you want and be gone for as long as you decide.

If you love winter weather, like to ski or just take in the sights of the snow and mountain landscape, rent a chalet in Verbier, Switzerland or enjoy the restaurants, spas and nightlife of Vail, Colorado.

Cabo San Lucas or Ibiza, Spain have become popular destinations for singles who are looking for other singles, the best margarita and sandy beaches. If you're searching for tranquility and seclusion, try the British Virgin Islands, Antigua or Belize.

Are you a history buff? You can see as many castles and ancient historic landmarks to your heart's delight throughout Europe. Imagine taking a Mediterranean cruise across the turquoise sea to ancient Greece.

Just do it if and when you can, pack light and don't forget the camera!

*Y*ou Stay Healthier

"You don't keep catching every cold and flu bug that your spouse, lover or roommate brings home."

Joe feels that he can finally breathe again after breaking up with his former girlfriend. *"Everything she had,"* he says, *"I caught."* He's certain that she picked up viruses at work. She's a school teacher and around kids all the time.

They had other differences, but mainly Joe believes that living single can deter a lot of problems. When he was in college, there was always someone sick in the dorm and where are you going to go? Where are you going to sleep? There's no escape.

Joe's not a geek about germs, but his point is well taken. If you share a space with someone, whether it's one or two rooms or an entire house, you're both susceptible to catching what the other one has.

$\mathcal{N}$o One Has to Witness Your Challenges If You're Disabled

Living alone, you're never embarrassed or humiliated if you're disabled. Managing a crippling disease robs you of your dignity and no one has to witness your toughest challenges in private.

If you're lucky to have a loved one that makes you feel at ease and helps you, regardless of what it takes, then you have won the lottery. If not, you're more comfortable dealing with it totally on your own, no matter how difficult it becomes.

For many, especially those who have been the caregivers before life dealt them a bad hand, it is more than just a physical challenge. It will beat you if you allow your emotions to get the best of you. Feeling sorry for yourself or crying will not make your legs move normally again or straighten your disfigured fingers.

You can't go back, but you can do amazing things for your spirit and general well being. You don't have to apologize for taking longer to get to the phone or finish in the bathroom. Even if life slows to a snail's pace, it's incredible what you learn and notice that you wouldn't have with your former healthy body.

On days when you strive for turning a negative into a positive, you find inner peace, stability and self worth. There will be those days when you'll have to accept the fact that you'll need to ask someone for help with something, but relish each moment you have been given, like a gift, as long as it lasts. Hold fast to your independence!

"Sometimes you have to stand alone to prove that you can still stand."

. . . Anonymous

There Are No Vultures Hovering Over Your Food

Reason #39

Ben says, *"Being single is all about the food, dude."* He loves the fact that he can be home, watching a game on TV and order an extra large pizza all for himself. As he's enjoying his meat lovers with extra cheese, no one is counting how many pieces are left. No pressure.

The days are over when someone else is worried about how much milk is left in the milk jug and that it's his fault that most of the milk is gone. He doesn't have to answer to anyone about why there are only a few crunched up pieces of potato chips in the bottom of the bag or why the last green pepper in the fridge has mold on it.

When Ben was a kid, he and his brother measured how much pop or milk was poured into their glasses. Now, there's no more measuring, counting or competition.

Um, excuse me, are you going to eat that?

You Can Come Home at Whatever Time You Like

Reason #38

Allison loves the fact that no one but you is watching the clock. When you're single, you can get home whatever time you like. If you stay out all night and come home at dawn-that is total independence, especially if there aren't hundreds of people leaving you phone messages wondering where you are. There is no one else to answer to but you.

If you want to hang at the library all day and study or put in some overtime at work, it only matters to you. There are those who are single and still have to deal with parents checking in on them, the kind of parents who just worry about their children.

Let's say you live in a big city. Your mother knows how long it takes to grocery shop, ride the subway, walk up ten flights of stairs, unload the bags and put everything away, or does she? She's just concerned for your safety. You'll have to forgive her. You may be a parent someday.

Along with the perks of single life, there are still those little things that are very important. If you're new to this and think you're finally free of living with mom, well, think again. Try to be responsible and considerate. Give yourself a few minutes. Take a deep breath and then call your mother!

*Y*ou Can Have the Couch All to Yourself

Andy admits that he doesn't mind being a couch potato. His life is all about sports. The couch, in addition to the television, are his best friends. His couch even has a name. He calls him 'Harry'.

When Andy wants to watch a game or flip around the channels and catch other games or events, he can do so freely without someone interrupting him or wanting to share a part of Harry the couch.

On Saturdays, everything happens there with Harry. Breakfast, lunch and dinner are served there, plus a snack or two in-between. It's just Andy, Harry, the coffee table and the TV. It doesn't get any better than that in Andy's mind.

Andy hopes the TV isn't mad since he hasn't given him a name. If he did, it would have to be a guy's name. He'll have to think about that later. He and Harry have a date!

You Can Take More Risks and Try New Things

Reason #36

Many will agree that the single lifestyle allows you more freedom to take risks and try new things, whatever your desire.

In 2009, a study at the University of Chicago revealed that women with higher testosterone levels were more likely to take financial risks. Luigi Zingales and his team tested the testosterone levels of more than 500 MBA students, (males and females), asking them to choose between a guaranteed monetary award and a risky lottery with a higher potential payout. Students had to choose repeatedly between the lottery and a fixed payment at increasing values.

In general, men with higher levels of testosterone were more likely to choose the risky lottery than women. Ironically, the women with higher levels of testosterone were almost seven times more likely to take risks than women with lower hormone levels.

In addition, the researchers found that married men and women had lower levels of testosterone than single individuals. Additionally, they noted that married people are also known to be more risk-averse than unmarried people.

$\mathcal{Y}$ou Can Have As Many Pets As You Want
Reason #35

Riley manages a pet rescue group in her home. She's been single for many years now and when she thinks of how nice it would be to have help with maintenance and care, that's not the reason to get married again.

Her ex-husband was an animal lover, but she knows he wouldn't have tolerated the tasks that her new life requires. The demands can be overwhelming at times. Unfortunately, because so many people have lost homes to foreclosure, they are abandoning their pets in Riley's own neighborhood. Many strays have showed up on her doorstep.

She's met many people who say that they would like to have a certain kind of cat or dog, but their spouse or roommate refuses to comply. The single life allows animal lovers countless freedoms. Fostering and caring for animals can change your life.

Please support your local animal rescue groups and shelters!

You Can Eat in Bed

Who can stop you from eating whatever you want, whenever you want . . . in bed?

You'll have a few crumbs to clean up, but who can resist? Granted, you still have to prepare it and transfer everything from the kitchen to your bedroom, but you can still enjoy one of life's simple pleasures.

A friend of mine said she missed her ex-boyfriend only because of one thing. He would bring her breakfast in bed. I said, *"What do you need him for? Treat yourself. You can even put a rose in a bud vase and place it on your tray."*

It's not exclusively about cookies and milk in bed either. From bean soup to spaghetti, a glass of wine or cup of hot cocoa, anything goes. Hopefully you won't spill the wine on your new white comforter.

Climb into bed now and aaah . . . doesn't that feel better?

There Are No Shoes to Trip Over

Reason #33

Erin grew up in a house with five brothers. Her mother was always asking, (yelling, actually), *"and who do these belong to?"* She rarely met with her mother's wrath over tidiness issues and recalls that her brothers never seemed to know whose shoes were whose, until someone finally gave in and put their shoes away in the required closet.

Erin wonders if it's exclusively a man thing. Her boyfriend has the same 'clutter gene' as her brothers. His shoes are always in her way, whether they're lying in the middle of the room or next to the bed. She asked him to leave his boots near the back door, but that plan failed miserably.

Now, Erin has turned into her mother, yelling, *"and who do these belong to?"*

You Can Focus More on School or Career

"Living alone, you're more apt to set the bar higher for yourself."

Some may view living single as a lonely life, but it is quite the opposite. It can be a blessing in disguise.

Flying solo, even on a temporary basis, can give you an opportunity to find what you're searching for and what you want from your life. It's a perfect time to take extra classes and further your education. Studying comes easier when your place is quiet and there are no interruptions.

Many career-minded singles find they can spend more time at work and chalk up a few extra points with the boss, while their married friends have to get home early or pick up the kids at daycare.

Dream, reach and improve. How high would you like to go?

You Don't Have to Listen to Him Hyperventilating Over Supermodels

Reason #31

Nicole's husband is obsessed with TV tabloid programs and cable news. Those have become his favorite channels now because of the Hollywood gossip reporters and scantily dressed super models and actresses. Even the cable news anchors wear blouses or sweaters with plunging necklines and skirts hiked up as far as their producers allow.

If you asked Nicole's husband what he misses most about being single, he would probably say the Playboy channel, but he's still got it made with regular cable.

One night, Nicole dressed in her favorite lingerie to cook dinner. When she started serving and asked him to come to the table, he practically pulled a muscle in his neck as he whipped around to catch another glance at a bombshell on the tube. You can't win!

You Rule!

Tina loves being single because she's queen of the castle. Every room is hers, every appliance, the car, the lawn mower and even the power tools. When important decisions are made, it all comes down to her and there are no discussions, arguments or debates.

If she's relaxing on the sofa and reading a good book, she doesn't have to get up and move if someone else wants to watch TV or take up the other end of the sofa. She sleeps when she wants to and sleeps in as late as she desires.

The noise in Tina's home is generated entirely by her. She can play her music as loud as she wants or enjoy total silence. Her bathroom, oh . . . the bathroom, don't get her started!

When you're single, You Rule!

"You have brains in your head. You have feet in your shoes. You can steer yourself in any direction you choose. You're on your own. And you know what you know. You are the guy who'll decide where to go."

. . . Dr. Seuss

You Can Talk To Yourself

Reason #29

I've discovered that I'm not shy when it comes to talking to myself. My cats and dogs are accustomed to me having one-sided conversations with them. I wish they could answer me back. Oh boy, how the truth would be revealed!

Most of the time, it's announcing what has to get done, what's coming up next or the usual self disciplinary cursing. I've said a few choice words while taking out the trash or checking the caller ID when telemarketers phone relentlessly.

When I lived in Manhattan, I remember seeing a man yelling at his soup in the neighborhood diner. He appeared a few weeks later on the street, yelling at the air and arguing with himself. A few days ago, I saw a woman talking loudly in her car, but I couldn't tell if she had a hands-free phone or if someone else was in the car that I couldn't see.

Talking to yourself comes easy in the privacy of your own home or car, but you have to be cautious not to continue the habit at the grocery store or when you're pumping gas. Hopefully, my neighbors never see me making a few choice comments when I go to the mailbox filled with bills.

No one answers back when you talk to yourself, but sometimes that's a good thing.

You Know Where the Soap Has Been
Reason #28

In an episode of the television sitcom, "Friends", the character Chandler says to his roommate Joey, *"If you take a shower after I do, what is the first thing you wash and what was the last thing I washed?"*

I shared a band house once in Boca Raton with a girl who played a solo gig at a local supper club. She would go to the beach everyday and leave sand in the tub after her shower. Luckily, she used her own soap.

Your roommate, your older brother, even your adorable wife or lover may share the same bar of soap with you. Who hasn't stepped into the shower and found black curly hairs all over the soap, the faucet and floor of the tub?

Now that you have that image in your mind, turn to a more inviting picture of your bathroom, your bath robe, your tub, your towels and you. You sink down into the tub and relax in the warmth of the bubble bath with your own fresh bar of soap.

You use liquid soap, you say? Now, there's a concept.

You Don't Have to Fake an Orgasm

Reason #27

Amanda just ended a three year relationship with someone that she really didn't enjoy being with, especially when it came to sex.

It was one of those flings at first, then something that grew into a boyfriend-girlfriend thing. One day, she realized that this was the person who figured he knew everything about her, especially when it came to intimacy. He knew nothing.

Maybe it was the way he kissed her or how it didn't feel like they were making love, she wasn't sure, but she couldn't wait for it to be over and so she faked every orgasm. What was she doing with this guy? She actually believed that she could eventually fall in love with him and her feelings would grow down the road, but she finally decided that it was never going to happen.

He was a nice guy and she feels bad that it was like lying to him, but for her now, it's great to be free and keeping it real.

No One Knows You Have Raggedy P.J.'s

Reason #26

One of my own comforts of home are my old pajamas. Several sets of tops and bottoms that have survived hundred of washes now have holes in places I don't need to mention. The older they get, the more comfortable they are and I can't throw them away.

Some pieces have eventually been sacrificed for dust cloths, but the others that keep hanging on, to my body that is, are like old friends and no one sees what I look like, as I sleep comfy and cozy.

When I was married, what I wore to bed was important and sometimes took planning. *"Why?"* I ask myself now. What a waste of time that was. After all that money invested in expensive lingerie and sexy nightwear, nothing is more uncomfortable than waking up in the middle of the night with garter clasps that have made permanent marks in my legs and push up bras that stopped pushing.

As I age along with my pajamas, I do wonder what if I die in my sleep and someone finds me sleeping in what appear to be rags. What will they think?

Comfort is key. Who's going to know? The rattier the better, since you're going to drool on them anyway.

*T*here is No Time Limit in the Bathroom

A toast to the single life and the time spent in the luxury of your own bath where you can spend all the time that you want. Who's going to set a timer?

Soak as long as you desire, paint your nails, pluck your eyebrows, hover over the heat register on a cold afternoon or fall asleep there on the floor. Camp on the commode and read a magazine until the skin of your thighs become glued to the toilet seat and you have to peel yourself away. Who cares?

Who is going to know about the smell, not matter how gross it gets? It doesn't matter if you have one, three or twelve bathrooms. No one is going to be knocking on the door, asking how much longer you will be. You don't even have to keep the door closed.

Most importantly, there is no pressure when you need your personal time with your mirror.

$\mathcal{Y}$ou Don't Have to be Afraid to Go it Alone

Reason #24

Single life is on the rise, according to the U.S. Census Bureau. In 2008, there were 92 million single Americans living in the states, where 54 percent were women and 63 percent had never been married. 14.5 million were unmarried or single, aged 65 and over. In the United Kingdom, there were 14.2 million singletons, aged 16-64.

Some say it's a social trend now to be single and living in Europe. Many feel that acquiring large sums of money is a greater priority than seeking a partner for life and more opportunities are available in Europe these days, after the lifting of borders.

Wherever you live there are countless organizations and groups who offer support to single men and women, no matter what your status or age. These are not just support groups or those who are in the matchmaking business. You can even start your own singles group in your community.

Don't allow fear or uncertainty to stand in your way.

*Y*ou Can Cut Your Grocery Bill in Half

Reason #23

How much do you think you could save on your grocery bill every month?

If you're currently putting out close to $600 every four weeks, that number could change dramatically if you're suddenly single, especially if the food expenses have been your part of the household budget plan for two adults.

Let's see how much you could save. Over the next twenty years, you could possibly save $75,000 or more. What a way to start saving for a rainy day! Could you use an extra $75k in twenty years?

Imagine all of your favorite goodies you could fill in your pantry! Not only can you now buy the food your spouse or roommate hated, but the stuff they loved and gobbled up before you had a chance to enjoy it.

Look at it this way, if gas prices continue to rise, the products at the market will go up accordingly. They say a gallon of milk will be close to $5.00 in the near future, so start saving your money and celebrate being single!

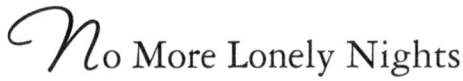
No More Lonely Nights

Reason #22

This is one of the most popular reasons among women. You don't have to worry about where he is, when he's coming home, who he is with or when he's going to call.

That stress is off your mind, off your shoulders and out from in-between your shoulder blades! Those scrunched up lines between your eyebrows are gone. The word, 'lonely' is not even a part of your vocabulary anymore.

There's no more disappointment when he forgets your birthday, an anniversary or blows off Valentine's Day.

There are no more lonely nights with him or without him.

*Y*ou Can Talk on the Phone as Long as You Like

Reason #21

Cara spends most of the day on the phone chatting and texting. She has a lot of friends and loves the fact that she can catch up with what's going on in life instantly. They don't miss a moment, sharing pics, schedules, scores, everything.

Her mom asks, *"What do you possibly have to talk about for hours on end?"* Oh, please! Guys, clothes and guys; shoes and guys; the latest gossip and guys. Duh!

Aren't you glad you don't have Cara's phone bill?

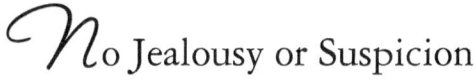

$\mathcal{N}$o Jealousy or Suspicion

Reason #20

Shelsa and her ex-husband met at a hospital where they both worked. He was an EMT working days and she was a nurse on duty at night. Their jobs were extremely stressful and both worked side by side with the opposite sex. Shelsa never worried once about him and always felt secure that he was true.

They married a couple of years later and before she knew it, he began acting suspicious about the new male interns who worked on her wing of the hospital. He was always asking her about who was on duty with her, if they had girlfriends or if they were married. Frankly, she didn't know that much about her male co-workers at all.

Finally, Shelsa confronted him about his jealousy and he flatly denied it. She told him that she needed for him to let go of his suspicions and trust her. *"If you have to ask me to trust you, then you must have something to hide,"* he replied.

Their marriage ended after five years. The stress created many days and weeks of unhappiness and wasted time.

"By persistently remaining single a man converts himself into a permanent public temptation."

. . . Oscar Wilde

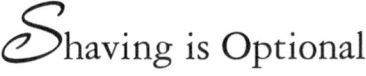

Shaving is Optional

"I shaved my legs for this?"

Nora thinks it's funny how the days go by as she procrastinates about shaving, especially when it comes to shaving her legs, in addition to her underarms. Since the time she was first allowed to shave her legs, she never missed a day. Now, she just laughs about it, knowing that no one is going to know or examine her up close.

If she's going out or dressing up, that's different, but just day after day after day is a waste of time and effort. She's lost count at how many times she's shaved when getting ready for a date and realized later that it wasn't necessary at all. It's just one more thing she can remove from the 'to do' list.

Paul believes that being single is less stressful because no one else uses your razor and you don't have to shave if you don't want to. On the weekends, he skips it and gives his skin a break. If he has a hot date, maybe he'll shave, maybe not.

$\mathcal{Y}$ou Can Hang Out at Home in Your Birthday Suit

Heather wishes she could walk around her house in her underwear, (or less), without it being considered an invitation.

Within the privacy of her own four walls, she wants to be comfortable. She sheds her work clothes and high heels after a long hard day at work as soon as she comes through the door. So she can finally breathe, the bra comes off too. There are days when she doesn't take the time to get fully dressed if chores need to get done, so she'll jump out of the shower, pull on her underwear and run the vacuum cleaner.

Her boyfriend seems to think that if she's scantily dressed while doing housework or cooking, it's an invitation to go to bed with him. When he sits around on Saturdays in his underwear watching the game, Heather doesn't view this as sensually suggestive, especially his boxer shorts with Spiderman on them.

Raise your glass to those singles who enjoy the freedom of the privacy of their own abode! Admit it. How many times have you checked your email naked?

You Are the Keeper of the Remote

If you're a woman and enjoying the single life, you can watch all the chick flicks you like. If you're a man, you can keep the games on 24/7. If television is your life, then one of best parts of being single is total control of the remote.

There are no battles over what to watch, who gets to watch what first, no trades, and no deals. The TV and the remote are all yours.

Most women can tell you that they know where the remote is at all times. Men may have to look under the cushions of the couch or behind the pizza box, but it's usually not far from being found.

Just imagine the war films, the soap operas and all the political talking heads you can stand. It never has to end, as long as you are the master of the remote.

The Smelly Socks Are Yours

Reason #16

Rachel was living with a guy who had the most disgusting dirty laundry she had ever seen. They split the household chores and laundry ended up being her responsibility, much to her dismay.

She imagined having a robot arm that could pick up his stinking socks and sweats. Wouldn't that be nice? It would grab everything from the laundry basket, swing around and drop it into the washing machine and hey, inventors, while you're at it, design a robot that will fold too!

The worst was his underwear. One day, Rachel told a friend that her boyfriend's briefs were always turned inside out in the hamper and every pair had brown stains, as if he scratched his rear end all the time. Her friend laughed and simply said, *"Those are called skid-marks!"* Rachel was even more disgusted after hearing that term and couldn't believe that she actually had sex with this guy- the guy with skid-marks.

Mr. Skid-Marks is out of the picture now and Rachel vows that she's staying single as long as she can. Just the other day, she reached into the hamper to pull out her not so white, fluffy socks. *"No, it can't be,"* she thought. The smelly socks were hers!

Kitchen Domination

Here are the top ten most popular reasons for enjoying your own kitchen:

1. No one else drinks the last gulp of milk or juice and puts the empty carton back into the fridge.

2. The dirty dishes in the sink are yours and will get washed when you're ready.

3. No one else is responsible for the limp celery in the fridge but you.

4. You can re-use the paper filter in the coffee maker.

5. You can lick the beater from the bowl of icing or taste-test the stew with the same spoon.

6. No one else changes the dark/light setting on the toaster.

7. You can double dip in the guacamole.

8. You can eat right out of the pan on the stove.

9. You're the only one who organizes the pantry.

10. It's no big deal if you burn the rice.

*F*arting is Less Embarrassing

Have you ever smiled when you opened up a can of beans because you knew that you wouldn't embarrass yourself later? You can make all the noise you want and enjoy the benefits as well.

Let's ponder the 'power' of beans, as it's really something to make noise about. Kidney, black, navy, pinto, garbanzo, soybeans and lentils are all low in fat, calories and sodium. High in fiber and the good carbs, they contain the Omega-6 fatty acids. Soybeans contain the Omega-3's. Studies have shown that if you add either canned or dry beans to your diet, you can reduce blood cholesterol levels by 10 percent within just two to three weeks.

Kidney beans alone are a good source of folate, potassium, iron, manganese, copper and zinc, known to aid in lowering blood pressure. In a study of almost 10,000 men and women, those who ate beans four or more times a week, cut their risk of coronary heart disease by nearly 20 percent, compared with those who ate beans less than once per week.

Beans and lentils have the same potent anti-inflammatory antioxidants, also found in teas, fruits, grapes, red wine and cocoa beans. It's interesting to note that the reddish flavonal pigments in bean and lentil seed coats exert antioxidant activity fifty times greater than vitamin E. They can protect against oxidative damage to cell membrane lipids; promote healthy collagen and cartilage; and restore the antioxidant powers of vitamins C and E after they've won their war over the free radicals.

So, man the guns mate, release those toxins and reap the benefits!

$\mathcal{T}$he Mattress is All Yours

Reason #13

Early in an intimate relationship, most couples rarely have a second thought about the size of their bed. They can easily fall asleep in each other's arms, but when the honeymoon's over, the struggle for space and personal comfort begins!

Tom and Nikki could fall asleep like two spoons for months after they were first married. Then, one night she woke up feeling like the left side of her head was wet and it was. He was slobbering on her! She told him that there were many things she loved about him, but that wasn't one of them.

Before they knew it, they were fighting for the covers, which side of the bed to sleep on and over who had the best pillow. Tom was even mad at her once because she jerked her leg in the middle of the night and woke him up from a wonderful dream.

Now, they want their own bedrooms!

o Toilet Lid Issues

Johanna was at a party with a group of friends one night and had to go to the bathroom. When she opened the bathroom door, she couldn't find the light switch. Keeping the door open just a crack, she went to sit on the john and literally fell in.

When she was growing up, her mom begged Johanna's brothers to put the lid down, but they thought it was enough to just put the seat down and not the lid as well. Johanna was accustomed to expecting the seat to be there, at least, but that night at the party was an awful experience and she was humiliated, to say the least.

Falling in was horrible enough. Leaving the door partially opened and everyone hearing her scream made it worse. She soon had her dignity back, but her friends will never let her forget about it.

In her own apartment, there are no toilet lid issues.

You Can Embrace the Unknown

How do we know when it's time to move on in order to realize our unfulfilled desires? Can we be certain when the time is right and if we're clearly interpreting our inner voice? When we allow doubt and fear to take control, our strongest desires, hopes and dreams are dashed.

Choosing to live the single life opens up far more opportunities to be spontaneous or make changes without drastically affecting a spouse or live-in partner. So much of a person's life can be lost and never replaced, due to the needs and decisions of a dominant spouse.

I was a radio talk show host, working the overnight shift at a radio station located fifty miles from my home. The journey to and from work would take close to an hour, one-way, six days per week. Each night, it was pitch black on the way in to work and on my return home, I would drive east into to the rising sun.

My husband and I had been married for just two years, but never shared the same schedule due to our jobs. I faced many challenges because of the hours that forced me to try to sleep during the day, but I was not alone in my struggle. Like my overnight audience, I was living on too much coffee and no sleep, not to mention any time at all with my husband and family.

One night on the way to work, I spied a new billboard along the highway with a black background and stark white letters that read, *"Embrace the Unknown!"* As I went on the air that night, I couldn't get the billboard off of my mind.

I opened up this question to my listeners, *"What would you do if you could change your life, right now?"* The phone lines in the studio lit up like a Christmas tree and the calls continued non-stop until the dawn. Along with my listeners, I heard unusual, bizarre and even funny ideas, yet those callers who went on the air, all had one thing in common- the desperation for independence, exhibiting the courage and desire to change their lives.

For another six months, I passed the billboard along the highway every night. The three simple words on the sign seemed to gain power, calling out to me rather than just invoking a thought. My reaction to the sign had finally evolved from the fear of what it was suggesting to the comfort in knowing that one can actually embrace their unknown future and just enjoy the journey.

During this period of time, my husband had been working feverishly to advance his own radio career, finally getting an offer, which meant transferring half-way across the United States. My husband flew to his interview and took the job, but didn't tell me in person. Instead, he called home and left a voicemail message. He said that he was taking the job and I would have to make arrangements to sell the house right away, in addition to giving my boss a notice that I'd be quitting. To say the least, I was disappointed that he didn't wait to share the final decision with me, his wife.

He returned home to close up some loose ends, and then packed for his trip to his new life. I'll never forget the day he drove out of the driveway, heading off into the horizon of his future. Standing there in the entrance of the front door of my house, I waved good-bye to him, thinking about the sign that read, *"Embrace the Unknown."*

I tried to believe with all my heart that I could do just that and support my husband. Another year later, I was moving again, only out of our apartment in Tallahassee and into my own place across town. I had lost my home that I had built with my dad, along with my job, which caused me to regress in my career. I struggled to find work in north Florida and southern Georgia without success and began to have panic attacks. My husband was dedicated to his new morning show and became distant, leaving me feeling lost and alone, far away from family and friends.

Soon diagnosed with rheumatoid arthritis, my doctor asked if I had been through a death in the family or a drastic change in my life. He claimed that traumatic events can bring auto-immune diseases to the surface. I believed that staying with my husband would be a greater challenge than having to deal with the disease, knowing that he was incapable of offering compassion and support. I asked him for a divorce and moved out.

As I carried the last box to my car, I thought of that day I stood in the doorway of my former home, watching him drive away. Though I should have had the courage to keep the house and tell him to go on without me, I now needed all the courage and strength I had left to embrace the unknown.

"Everything that irritates us about others can lead us to an understanding of ourselves."
. . . Carl Jung

*Y*ou Don't Have to Worry About Morning Breath

If you suddenly find yourself in a relationship and have moved in together, you've got to be on your toes now. You are not alone in the morning and two things will remain- morning hair and morning breath.

Did you take the time to remove your makeup last night? Will your hair be matted from all the hairspray you used the day before? Even if you brushed your teeth before you went to bed, you won't be minty fresh when the alarm goes off.

The man you wake up next to doesn't have it any easier, even if he thinks he looks like an Adonis. How many of us have tried to wake up before our lover to slip into the bathroom and squeeze a little toothpaste into our mouths and swish it around?

It can become nerve-racking trying to live like that, but it usually doesn't last long. Either the two of you don't care anymore or you've returned to the single life, not having to worry about it anymore.

No Extra Work When You Come Home from Work

Reason #9

According to Tara, being single is being able to come home from work and not start working all over again. She has lived with three different boyfriends. Each relationship started out as if it was going to last forever and every time, she convinced herself that she'd found Mr. Right. Now, she's Ms. Wrong, but grateful that she doesn't have to come home and become someone else's slave.

Wouldn't it be great to find someone who might have dinner ready for you when you came through the door at night or someone who decided it would be thoughtful to walk the dog or throw a load of clothes in the washer before you got home?

In most of these relationships, the guy doesn't seem to realize there might be more time to spend together if he helped around the house occasionally. Fortunately now for Tara, she finds her house the way she left it when she comes home.

$\mathcal{Y}$our Middle Name Isn't 'Maid Service'

Reason #8

Every time I have found myself between relationships or when I was just divorced and on my own, the greatest relief has always been the fact that there is no more cleaning up after a man. I'm a fussy housekeeper and I would just like for the floor to stay clean for at least thirty minutes after I've scrubbed and waxed. Thirty minutes isn't much to ask for, but if you're living with a messy, inconsiderate person, they win, you lose.

I should have done a better job at paying attention to the signals early on in most of these relationships. My second husband's apartment was abominable. Every item of clothing he had worn for two weeks was all over the bedroom floor of his apartment. He wasn't worried about it at all and said that everything got picked up when it was time to go to the Laundromat. Each morning, he would have a bowl of cereal in plastic gray bowls saved from his childhood. When he was finished drinking the remaining milk, he would sit the bowl down anywhere in the apartment. There were cereal bowls with spoons stuck in them, haphazardly left in every room.

You ask, *". . . and you married this guy?"* Well, yeah. It was another one of those relationships where you love someone so much, you convince yourself that they will change. Don't be a fool!

No More Broken Hearts

When another Valentine's Day approaches, I applaud those couples who are truly in love and celebrating their happiness and commitment to each other.

For millions out there, life has only offered up disappointment and whether you have broken other hearts or had your own broken, the question wanes, *"Will I ever find true love?"*

As time goes on, flying solo becomes so comfortable and free. At the very least, there is no more despair over what was once an intimate, loving relationship. You do find happiness with loving friends and family.

Our hearts can still be broken when we learn of others in trouble or in pain or of an orphaned child we cannot reach or help. Life can break our hearts.

Yet, hearts can be mended with love and kindness. By giving to others, your own heart will heal.

No More Physical Abuse

Elaine fears that the man she lies next to in bed is a threat to her well being. She promises herself that one day she will finally be free from him. Some people ask her what she is waiting for, but she believes she has to protect her children and they come first. As soon as she finds the right people she can really trust and the place where she feels safe, she will make her move.

She had transferred to Tuscon with her husband because of his job. She misses home back east and hopes to return there someday. When she met her husband, she thought he was a sweetheart. He comes from a good family, but his own mother and sister don't understand him now. Maybe it has been the stress from his job that has changed him, who can really say?

Elaine finally found a job about a year after they moved to Arizona. The longer it took, the more her husband began to doubt that she was trying hard enough to find work. She's a receptionist for a marketing group and there are a lot of single people who work there. She's had to cover up a black eye with makeup, wear long sleeved shirts to cover bruises on hot days and running out of excuses when people ask her what has happened and if she's okay.

Her quest is to be single again, even though it means being a single mother. She has met several single moms from her daughter's school who strongly encourage other women who are suffering from abuse to not be afraid to go it alone.

You Don't Have to Tolerate Someone Else's Annoying Habits

Reason #5

If Jen ever considers living with someone again, a few of the critical questions she will focus on will be:

1. What if they're a smoker or they do drugs?
2. What if they're a religious fanatic?
3. Can I deal with them constantly talking on their cell or texting?
4. What if he's a mama's boy?
5. What if he's a cave man and has never lived with someone before?
6. Does he have job security?
7. Is he healthy?

Jen came very close to living with a guy who she soon discovered was a hypochondriac. If he heard about a new virus, he decided that he definitely had it too. He claimed to be allergic to so many things, she didn't know how he dealt with life in general.

He had boxes of tissues in every room of his apartment and hand sanitizer in his pocket. She went to the movie theater with him one night and he insisted on wiping the door handles on his own car.

That was enough for her. She broke it off before she started doing mean things like cleaning out his medicine cabinet.

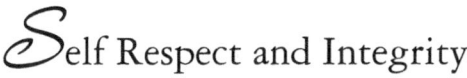elf Respect and Integrity

Reason #4

You get to know who you really are, gain more self respect, confidence and self worth when you're faced with life alone. Studies have shown that the essence of your self esteem shines brighter when you have given yourself the opportunity of living single, even if it's for a temporary period in your life.

Making important decisions on your own that directly affect your future builds confidence and self respect. How you handle living alone and taking charge of your own life can reveal who you truly are, allowing more growth and development in a positive way.

The single life is easier for those with independent personalities and perfect for fearless, creative and passionate minds. Those who consider themselves meek or dependent upon others will most likely fail at flying solo.

If given a try, you'll discover pride and integrity.

$\mathcal{Y}$ou Manage Your Own Finances

Reason #3

When you're single, the scales can tip either way. If you have a lot of money it's all yours to keep and the bills are your responsibility if you're in debt.

If you mess up your financial plan, make stupid mistakes in your checkbook ledger, the monkey is on your back. You are the one who has to fix it, find it and save it. No one is to blame but you. If you're successful, pat yourself on the back and enjoy the fruits of YOUR labor.

After my first divorce, I changed my last name back to my maiden name. If I would have known that it was not a wise decision at that time, I wouldn't have made it. Suddenly it was as if I had never existed before. All of the money I had worked so hard for and saved with my first husband didn't matter. There was no such thing as a credit history in my maiden name.

Consideration has to be made as well for the fact that this was the late 1970's. When I tried to get a loan to buy a car, I had several strikes against me. I was a woman, recently divorced, a musician and had no credit history.

Today, you decide how you'll manage and pay for your credit cards, apply for a home mortgage, buy a car, travel and more. Hopefully, you can live within your budget and enjoy what you've saved. After taxes, it's all yours!

mpowerment

Kristi discovered that her husband was having an affair. She demanded that they get a divorce, placing herself in a position where she needed a new place to live, a car to drive, and a job. She didn't want any part of what had been theirs together.

She was devastated and petrified, as her husband had always been the bread winner in the family. They had never had children, but for the first time in her life, Kristi was faced with being responsible for her own survival.

In just six months, she found a great job, acquired her first credit card and apartment lease in her own name. Years later, she continued her education toward a degree, traveled to Europe and took a cruise, achieving more in five years of being single than she did in fifteen years of marriage.

$\mathcal{L}$oneliness Can be Much Greater with Someone Than Without

Reason #1

For almost four years, I dated a man who was ten years younger. We lived together for three. After the first year, I became disenchanted and frequently pondered about how much happier I am when I'm living alone.

We were clinging to each other for financial support and security, but romance dissipated rapidly. Eventually, I chose to transfer out of town, buying my own home and he moved to another apartment. For another year, we visited each other on weekends and during the holidays. I will always be grateful to him for his compassion and support when my father passed away. However, neither of us had the courage to come to the table nor verbally commit to ending our relationship, which was strange in so many ways.

One day I received an invitation to attend a concert at a local college and I emailed him to see if he might be interested in joining me. He said that he would like to go and we agreed to touch base as the concert date drew near. The day before the concert, I called to see if he was still planning to go. He said that he was, but that there was something he had better tell me first.

To sum it all up, he had met someone over a year prior to this and they were married in Germany. I laughed out loud, thinking he was kidding, in addition to the fact that I had always been certain he was a confirmed bachelor for life. His bride was still stuck in Europe, going through immigration red tape. We attended the concert, visited like two old friends over dinner and then never saw each other again.

One week after the concert, in the middle of one of the coldest nights of that winter, my furnace broke down. It was two below zero and the temperature inside my house was falling rapidly through the wee hours of the morning. As I sat huddled over my space heater, replaying the events of recent weeks in my head, I came to realize that whether my boyfriend was still with me or not, I would be the one dealing with the furnace problem. In those early hours of that brutally, frigid February morning, I decided to write this book and launch the *Single 101* blog.

It's been a roller coaster ride of emotions, remembering the love lost over both of my marriages and the men who temporarily played the role of Mr. Right in my life.

I still remain with the same conclusion, time and time again, *"It's far better to be alone than to wish you were."*

The Secret to a Long and Happy Life

Bonus Reason

My grandfather, Wilfred Powell, told me once that he drank a cup of hot water with vinegar and honey every day. He claimed that it gave him energy and stamina. Gregory Nestor, one of the world's oldest humans, credits his longevity to barefoot walks, sour milk and never being married.

Centenarians share many similarities with healthy habits, including exercise, strength training, diet and stress reduction. Many believe that being socially active is the key to a long life and studies have shown that they experience less depression, have stronger immune systems and a lower incidence of heart disease.

Dr. Maoshing Ni, who specializes in tai chi and longevity offers such tips as eating more blueberries, telling the truth and saying 'no' to undue burdens. He believes there are hundreds of proven ways to make everyone's stay on earth much happier.

$\mathcal{S}$INGLE 101 QUIZ

To see if you'd be happy living the single life, take this short quiz:

1. *How well do you handle being alone?*
   a. no problem
   b. feel lonely sometimes
   c. miss people being around

2. *Are the holidays stressful without someone in your life?*
   a. I go out and share it with friends or volunteer
   b. not at all, just another day
   c. yes, it's very sad and melancholy

3. *Are you lonesome eating alone?*
   a. no, I enjoy the serenity at my dinner table
   b. sometimes, but I'll eat while watching television
   c. yes, I order a lot of pizzas

4. *Do you prefer to have the bed all to yourself?*
   a. absolutely!
   b. it doesn't really make any difference
   c. I wish I had someone to cozy up to

5. *How comfortable are you with being a Ms. vs. a Mrs.?*
   a. very comfortable
   b. it doesn't matter
   c. I miss being someone's wife

6. *Can you multi-task at home on your own?*
   a. yes
   b. sometimes
   c. I hire some of it to be done

7. *How easy is it for you to organize your own schedule?*
   a. very easy
   b. it depends on how much I have to do
   c. I feel guilty if I'm not taking care of someone else

8. *For you, being single is:*
   a. choosing not to be in a relationship
   b. living without someone to love
   c. ending up like a spinster/confirmed bachelor

9. *When your friends announce their engagements, you are:*
   a. thrilled for them
   b. feel slightly jealous
   c. feel like a loser

10. *Family and friends keep asking if you're seeing someone. What do you tell them?*
    a. the truth
    b. try to change the subject
    c. start to cry

11. *Another couple asks you to join them out for an evening. Do you . . .*
    a. go and have a great time
    b. decide not to go because 'three's a crowd'
    c. make an excuse why you can't go

12. *You bump into an attractive person on the street and your eyes meet. You . . .*
    a. don't think anything of it
    b. wish you weren't such a klutz
    c. wish that he/she was attracted to you

13. *How often do you think of when you were married or dating someone?*
    a. almost never
    b. not often
    c. every day

14. *Being the only single person in a group of couples is . . .*
    a. something I don't even notice
    b. makes me wish I had someone too
    c. extremely uncomfortable

15. *If you've been single for a while, you . . .*
    a. start meeting new people and finding new interests
    b. feel a bit confused and lonely, but keep busy
    c. are lost and starved for affection

16. *On a typical Friday or Saturday night you . . .*
    a. find time to enjoy reading a book, watch a movie or catch up on your rest
    b. decide that going out isn't worth the time and trouble
    c. miserable and wishing you had someplace to go

17. *Do you have good friends, a career you enjoy, and other interests?*
    a. absolutely!
    b. I have some of those things
    c. not really

18. *Do you enjoy shopping for one at the grocery or market?*
    a. definitely, because I buy whatever I want
    b. it's sometimes difficult to buy for only one person
    c. I try to avoid it, as it reminds me of how alone I am

19. *While in a relationship, have you ever wished that you were on your own?*
    a. yes, most of the time
    b. sometimes
    c. never

20. *If planning a vacation right now, would you be making reservations for one?*
    a. maybe, but I might ask a friend to join me
    b. not sure, but I might to save money
    c. no, I'd prefer to stay at home if I'm all alone

If you answered:
'a' to most of the questions, you can definitely handle flying solo.
50% 'a' and 50% 'b', you'll be able to survive.
Mostly 'b', you are on the fence whether or not to remain single.
Mostly 'c', you may struggle and find it difficult coping with the single life.

$\mathcal{A}$uthor Biography . . .

The granddaughter of a big band leader, Celeste began at a very young age as a student of the piano. Her musical career developed after she joined her first band, touring the United States in nightclubs and showrooms, followed by a career in broadcasting as an on-air talent and program director. During this period, she developed her writing skills as a copywriter for radio and scriptwriter for television in the early 1980's. For the past fifteen years, she has focused on her career as a singer-songwriter, composer, producer and voice talent.

A 2005 Grammy® nominee and the winner of the 2005 Ohioana Library Association's Citation Award in Music and Education, Friedman is also a two-time Pat Weaver Award nominee for her contributions in television and has been nominated twice for the Indie Artist of the Year Award in The Netherlands. Her national credits include Live! with Regis and Kelly, A Prairie Home Companion, Public Radio International, Music Choice, the ESPN Network and Blog Talk Radio.

In the mid 1990's, Celeste began writing songs, books and plays for children and has published an extensive catalog of albums and self-published books in the children's category. As a composer, she writes for television, film and animation, scoring for such great productions as the Pulitzer Prize nominated play, *"The Glory of Living."*

Known as a prolific singer-songwriter and passionate performer, Ms. Friedman currently produces from her own recording studio. Her music is heard globally, reaching Number One on the European Country Music charts in 2007 with her album, *"Every Tear I Know."* One of the ballads from that CD, *"Wild Horses,"* was selected to be a part of a compilation CD, *"All States All Stars,"* delivered to our troops in Iraq and Afghanistan. In 2009, Music for Troops selected Celeste again for their CD compilation, *"Operation 11.11.09,"* adding her ballad, *"A Home Run."* Her compositions have been featured in several national and international film festivals throughout the United States and Canada, including the Ottawa International Animation Festival in Canada in 2007 and Festival de Cannes in 2008.

Celeste's discography includes the following albums: *"Every Tear I Know"*, *"Live at the Bluebird Café"*, *"The Tide"*, *"Sweet Magnolia Wine"*, *"The Road to Santiago" and "Single 101"* with several selections available on CD Baby and iTunes. Compilations include: *"One to Grow On"*, *"All States All Stars" and "Operation 11.11.09"*

Celeste has been enjoying the single life for several years, but she's never alone. She shares her home and studio in Ohio with a few cats and dogs in the world of *Songs For Charlie Music.*

Learn more about her music and writings at the following links:

www.SongsForCharlieMusic.com
www.16Crayons.com
www.MySpace.com/celestefriedman
www.MySpace.com/songsforcharliemusic
www.Single-101.blogspot.com

"I think, therefore I'm single."
. . . Liz Winston